Practical CSS: Develop Real-World Websites with Modern Styling Techniques

BETTA D. RANDELL

Contents

Introduction: Why Practical CSS?

Welcome aboard! If you're holding this book, chances are you've seen the web, you've maybe tinkered with some HTML, and now you're looking at how to make things look... well, good! And not just good in a static image, but good on your phone, good on your desktop, good for everyone. You're ready to dive into CSS.

Now, CSS, or Cascading Style Sheets, sometimes gets a bit of a reputation. Some see it as just the "paint" layer of the web – the stuff that makes buttons round or text red. They might think it's less complex or less important than JavaScript or backend code. If you've ever felt that way, or if you've ever tried to center a `div` and felt like you were fighting an invisible force field, you're in good company.

But here's the truth: **Modern CSS is incredibly powerful and fundamental to building *any* successful website or web application today.** It's not just about colors and fonts anymore (though it does that beautifully). It's about layout, responsiveness, accessibility, performance, and creating truly engaging user experiences. Think about it – a user's very first impression of your project is visual. How it looks and feels *matters*.

This book isn't about just memorizing properties. It's about taking a **practical approach** to CSS. We're going to focus on how to use CSS *right now*, to build real-world websites and components that are robust, responsive, and maintainable. We'll cover the essential foundations, yes, but quickly move into the modern techniques that professional developers use every single day.

The Role of CSS in Today's Web Development

So, let's redefine the role of CSS. It's the language that tells the browser *how* to present your content. And in modern web development, this presentation layer is responsible for far more than just aesthetics:

- **Layout:** Gone are the days of struggling with floats and clearing. Modern CSS with Flexbox and CSS Grid gives us incredibly powerful, flexible, and intuitive ways to arrange elements on a page, from simple forms to complex dashboard layouts.
- **Responsiveness:** With the explosion of devices (phones, tablets, desktops, smartwatches, TVs!), your website needs to look and function well everywhere. Media Queries are the cornerstone of making your designs adapt gracefully to different screen sizes.
- **Accessibility:** A crucial part of responsible web development is ensuring your site can be used by *everyone*, including those with disabilities. CSS plays a key role here, from ensuring sufficient color contrast to managing focus states and visual hierarchy.
- **Performance:** Believe it or not, how you write and organize your CSS can significantly impact how fast your website loads and renders. We'll touch on best practices to keep your styles lean and efficient.

- **User Experience (UX):** Subtle animations, smooth transitions, clear visual feedback on interactions – these are all crafted with CSS and contribute significantly to how a user feels when interacting with your site.

CSS is the crucial link between your HTML structure and the final visual experience. It works hand-in-hand with JavaScript frameworks like React, Vue, or Angular, or even just plain HTML, to bring interfaces to life. A strong understanding of CSS makes you a much more valuable and versatile developer, regardless of your preferred JavaScript flavor.

What You Will Learn and Who This Book is For

This book is designed for anyone who wants to gain a confident, practical understanding of CSS for building modern websites.

- **Are you new to CSS?** Great! We'll start with the absolute basics, building up your knowledge step by step. We'll explain the core concepts like selectors, the cascade, and the box model in clear, simple terms.
- **Do you know some CSS but struggle with layout and responsiveness?** Perfect! We'll dedicate significant time to mastering Flexbox and CSS Grid, the game-changers for modern layout, and show you how to build truly responsive designs with Media Queries.
- **Are you a developer primarily focused on JavaScript (like React) but feel your CSS skills are holding you back?** You're exactly who this book is for! We'll focus on the CSS concepts that translate directly to component-based development, helping you style your applications effectively.
- **Do you want to move beyond theoretical examples and build actual things?** That's our core philosophy! We'll include numerous practical examples and guide you through building several real-world mini-projects.

By the end of this book, you won't just know *about* CSS properties; you'll know *how* and *when* to use them effectively to solve common web design challenges. You'll be able to take a design idea and confidently translate it into working, responsive, and well-structured CSS.

Setting Up Your Workspace: Tools and Environment

One of the great things about learning CSS is that the setup is incredibly simple. You don't need complex databases or servers to get started.

Here's what you'll need:

1. **A Code Editor:** This is where you'll write your HTML and CSS code. There are many excellent, free options available. Visual Studio Code (VS Code) is a popular choice in the web development community due to its features and extensions, and it's what I personally use and recommend. Sublime Text and Atom are other great alternatives. Choose one you feel comfortable with.
2. **A Web Browser:** You'll need a modern web browser to view your work. Chrome, Firefox, Safari, and Edge are all excellent. Crucially, they all come with built-

in **Developer Tools** (often accessed by right-clicking on a page element and selecting "Inspect" or by pressing F12). These tools are *your best friend* for learning and debugging CSS. You can see which styles are applied, where they come from, and even experiment with changes directly in the browser.

That's it! You'll typically work with two main file types: `.html` for structure and `.css` for styles. You simply link your CSS file to your HTML file, open the HTML file in your browser, and start coding. For the initial chapters, this simple setup is all you need. As we progress into projects, we might touch upon slightly more involved setups (like using a simple local server or implicitly using build tools via framework examples), but the core CSS concepts remain the same.

Personal Insight: Learning to effectively use browser developer tools was a game-changer for me. Don't just look at your page; *inspect* it. See which CSS rules are affecting an element, play with values, disable rules. It's the fastest way to understand the cascade and troubleshoot layout issues. Make it a habit from day one!

Embracing Practical, Project-Based Learning

Theory is important, but CSS is a skill best learned by doing. That's why this book is structured around a **practical, project-based approach**.

Instead of isolated examples for each property, we'll often combine concepts to build small, functional pieces of a website. We'll walk through code step-by-step, explaining not just *what* a property does, but *why* we're using it in a specific context and how it fits into the bigger picture of the design.

The later chapters are dedicated entirely to building larger, more complex projects. This is where you'll solidify your knowledge, face real-world challenges (like cross-browser quirks or integrating different layout techniques), and build a portfolio of practical examples.

I strongly encourage you to type out the code examples yourself. Don't just copy and paste. The physical act of typing, making mistakes, and fixing them is a powerful way to reinforce learning. Experiment! Change values, remove properties, see what happens. Break things – that's often how you learn the most.

It won't always be easy. There will be moments of frustration when something doesn't look quite right. Every developer has faced the infamous "centering a div" puzzle! But stick with it. The feeling of satisfaction when a complex layout finally snaps into place, or when your design fluidly adapts to different screen sizes, is incredibly rewarding.

We've got a lot of exciting stuff to cover, from the foundational principles to the latest features that make CSS so powerful today. So, get your code editor ready, open up your browser, and let's build some beautiful, practical websites together!

Chapter 1: CSS Fundamentals: The Building Blocks

Welcome to the starting point of your CSS journey! Before we get into exciting layouts, dazzling colors, and smooth animations, we need to understand the language itself. Just like any language, CSS has its own syntax, its own way of addressing elements, and its own set of rules for how styles are processed. Getting these fundamentals down solid will make everything else we cover much, much easier.

Let's break it down into digestible pieces.

1.1 Understanding CSS Syntax: Rules, Declarations, and Statements

At its most basic level, CSS consists of **rules**. A CSS rule (often called a ruleset) is like a single instruction telling the browser: "Find these specific HTML elements, and then apply these styles to them."

A rule is made up of two main parts:

1. The **Selector**: This is the part that targets the HTML elements you want to style.
2. The **Declaration Block**: This contains one or more declarations, enclosed in curly braces {}.

Inside the declaration block, you have one or more **declarations**. Each declaration is a pair consisting of a **property** and a **value**, separated by a colon :, and ending with a semicolon ;.

Think of it like this:

```
selector {
property: value;
property: value;
...
}
```

Let's look at a simple example:

```
/* This is a CSS rule */
p {                /* This is the selector (targets all <p> elements) */
  color: blue;   /* This is a declaration (property: color, value:
blue) */
  font-size: 16px; /* This is another declaration */
}                  /* End of the declaration block */
```

In this rule:

*   p is the **selector**. It tells the browser to find all paragraph (<p>) elements on the page.
*   { ... } is the **declaration block**.

- `color: blue;` is a **declaration**. The `color` property sets the text color to `blue`.
- `font-size: 16px;` is another **declaration**. The `font-size` property sets the text size to `16` pixels.

Key Takeaways:

- Every style instruction is a **rule**.
- A rule starts with a **selector** to pick elements.
- The styles are listed in a **declaration block** (`{ }`).
- Each style instruction within the block is a **declaration**, made of a **property** and a **value** (`property: value;`).
- Don't forget the semicolon `;` at the end of each declaration! (The last one in a block is technically optional, but it's good practice to always include it).

That's the fundamental syntax you'll see repeated throughout every CSS file. Simple, right?

1.2 Selectors: Targeting HTML Elements Effectively (Type, Class, ID, Attribute)

Okay, we know the syntax, but the *most* important part of a rule is the selector. How do we tell the browser exactly which elements to style? CSS gives us several ways to target elements, from broad strokes to very specific ones.

Here are the most common types you'll use daily:

1. Type (or Element) Selectors:

These are the simplest. They target all instances of a specific HTML tag.

```
/* Selects ALL <h1> elements */
h1 {
  color: darkcyan;
}


/* Selects ALL button elements */
button {
  cursor: pointer;
}
```

- **Use case:** Applying base styles to all elements of a certain type (e.g., setting default font for `body`, default list style for `ul`).

2. Class Selectors:

These are incredibly versatile and probably the selectors you'll use the most. They target all elements that have a specific `class` attribute. In your HTML, you add a `class="class-name"` attribute to an element. In CSS, you target it using a dot (`.`) followed by the class name.

```html
<!-- HTML -->
<p class="intro-text">Welcome!</p>
<div class="card">...</div>
<button class="primary-button">Click Me</button>
<button class="secondary-button">Cancel</button>
```

```css
/* CSS */
/* Selects any element with the class "intro-text" */
.intro-text {
  font-style: italic;
}


/* Selects any element with the class "primary-button" */
.primary-button {
  background-color: steelblue;
  color: white;
}


/* Selects any element with the class "secondary-button" */
.secondary-button {
  background-color: lightgray;
}
```

- **Use case:** Applying reusable styles to multiple elements across your site (e.g., styles for different button types, card styles, text highlighting). Elements can have multiple classes (e.g., `<button class="primary-button large">`).

3. ID Selectors:

These target an element with a specific `id` attribute. In HTML, you add an `id="id-name"` attribute (which *should* be unique on the *entire page*). In CSS, you target it using a hash (`#`) followed by the ID name.

```html
<!-- HTML -->
<div id="site-header">...</div>
<main id="main-content">...</main>
<!-- Avoid using IDs for styling elements you might repeat, like
buttons -->
```

```css
/* CSS */
/* Selects the single element with the ID "site-header" */
#site-header {
  border-bottom: 1px solid #ccc;
}
```

- **Use case:** Targeting a single, unique element on a page (like a header, footer, or main content area).
- **Important Note:** While IDs *can* be used for styling, they have very high "specificity" (we'll talk about that next!). This high specificity makes them hard to override with other styles later. For this reason, it's often recommended to use classes for styling whenever possible and reserve IDs for JavaScript hooks or page anchors.

4. Attribute Selectors:

These are more specific. They target elements based on the presence or value of a particular HTML attribute.

```html
<!-- HTML -->
<input type="text" placeholder="Enter name">
<input type="submit" value="Send">
<a href="#section-a">Go to Section A</a>
<img src="logo.png" alt="Company Logo">
/* CSS */
/* Selects all input elements with type="text" */
input[type="text"] {
  border: 1px solid blue;
}


/* Selects all elements with a 'data-modal-open' attribute (regardless
of value) */
[data-modal-open] {
  cursor: zoom-in;
}


/* Selects all <a> elements whose href attribute STARTS WITH "#" */
a[href^="#"] {
  font-weight: bold;
}
```

- **Use case:** Styling form elements based on their type, targeting custom data attributes (like data-*), or styling links based on their destination.

There are many more selector types and combinations (descendant selectors, child selectors, adjacent sibling selectors, pseudo-classes like :hover, :focus, :nth-child, etc.), but mastering Type, Class, ID, and Attribute selectors will give you the power to target most elements you need.

1.3 The Cascade, Specificity, and Inheritance Explained

This section is where things can sometimes feel a bit mysterious, but understanding these core concepts is absolutely vital to debugging CSS issues and predicting which styles will apply.

Imagine you have multiple style rules that all apply to the same element. How does the browser decide which rule "wins"? This is where the **Cascade**, **Specificity**, and **Inheritance** come into play.

The Cascade:

The word "Cascading" in CSS isn't just for show! It refers to the process by which the browser combines styles from different sources:

1. **Browser Default Styles:** Every browser has its own built-in stylesheet that provides default styling for HTML elements (e.g., headings are bold and large, links are blue and underlined).
2. **User Stylesheets (Optional):** Users can set up their own stylesheets in their browser preferences, often for accessibility reasons (like forcing a minimum font size).
3. **Author Styles (Your CSS!):** This is the CSS you write and link to your HTML.
4. **!important Rules:** Declarations marked with `!important` have a special, high priority (more on this in Specificity).

The cascade flows from less important sources to more important ones. Your "Author Styles" generally override the browser defaults. If there's a conflict *within* your Author Stylesheet, the browser uses Specificity to decide.

Specificity:

This is the browser's tie-breaking system. When multiple CSS rules target the *same* element and define the *same* property (like `color`), the rule with the *highest specificity* wins.

Think of it like a scoring system, though you don't need to calculate exact numbers initially. Just understand the hierarchy:

- **Inline Styles (`<p style="color: red;">`):** Styles applied directly to an HTML element using the `style` attribute. These have the highest specificity (excluding `!important`).
- **IDs (`#my-id`):** The next highest specificity.
- **Classes (`.my-class`), Attribute Selectors (`[type="text"]`), and Pseudo-classes (`:hover`, `:focus`):** These have medium specificity.
- **Element/Type Selectors (`p`, `div`, `h1`) and Pseudo-elements (`::before`, `::after`):** These have low specificity.
- **Universal Selector (`*`):** The lowest specificity.

Example of Specificity:

```
/* Style 1: Low Specificity (Element Selector) */
p {
  color: blue;
}


/* Style 2: Medium Specificity (Class Selector) */
.red-text {
  color: red;
}


/* Style 3: High Specificity (ID Selector) */
#main-paragraph {
  color: green;
}
```
```html
<!-- HTML -->
<p class="red-text" id="main-paragraph">This paragraph has styles.</p>
```
Which color will the paragraph be?

1. The `p` rule applies (targets `<p>`). Color is blue.
2. The `.red-text` rule applies (targets element with class `red-text`). Color is red.
3. The `#main-paragraph` rule applies (targets element with ID `main-paragraph`). Color is green.

The browser looks at the selectors: `#main-paragraph` (ID) has higher specificity than `.red-text` (Class), which has higher specificity than `p` (Element). Therefore, the `#main-paragraph` rule wins, and the text will be **green**.

If you had an inline style like `<p style="color: purple;" class="red-text" id="main-paragraph">`, the inline style would win, making the text purple.

The `!important` Flag:

You can add `!important` after a value to give that *specific declaration* even higher precedence than regular specificity rules.

```
.my-element {
  color: blue !important; /* This rule will win over almost everything else */
}
```
Personal Insight: While `!important` seems like a quick fix, it's often a sign that your specificity or CSS organization is becoming hard to manage. Relying on `!important` is generally frowned upon because it breaks the natural flow of the cascade and makes it very difficult to

override those styles later, leading to CSS spaghetti. Try to avoid it unless absolutely necessary (e.g., sometimes for overriding third-party library styles in specific, limited cases).

Inheritance:

Some CSS properties are automatically passed down ("inherited") from a parent element to its children. This is super convenient for things like text styles.

- **Properties that typically inherit:** `color`, `font-family`, `font-size`, `font-weight`, `line-height`, `text-align`, `list-style`, etc.
- **Properties that typically *do not* inherit:** `border`, `margin`, `padding`, `width`, `height`, `background-color`, `display`, `position`, etc. (These are usually specific to the element itself).

Example of Inheritance:

```css
/* CSS */
body {
  font-family: 'Arial', sans-serif;
  color: #333;
}


.my-div {
  border: 1px solid red; /* This will NOT be inherited by the
paragraph */
}
```
```html
<!-- HTML -->
<body>
  <div class="my-div">
    <p>This is a paragraph inside a div.</p>
  </div>
</body>
```

The paragraph inside the `div` will inherit the `font-family` and `color` from the `body`. So, its text will be Arial and dark gray. However, it will *not* inherit the red border from the `div`.

Understanding the cascade, specificity, and inheritance is like understanding how rules and family traits work together. It helps you predict why a style is or isn't being applied and how to fix it.

1.4 The Box Model: Content, Padding, Border, and Margin

Alright, let's talk about the fundamental structure of HTML elements from a CSS perspective. In CSS, *every* element is treated as a rectangular **box**. Even things that don't look like boxes, like text or images, live inside these conceptual boxes.

The standard CSS Box Model describes how the space an element occupies is calculated, based on four layers (from innermost to outermost):

1. **Content Box:** This is the area where your actual content sits – your text, an image, etc. Its dimensions are primarily determined by the `width` and `height` properties you set (though content can overflow if not managed).

2. **Padding Box:** This is the space *between* the content and the border. Padding pushes the border away from the content. You control it with the `padding` properties (`padding-top`, `padding-right`, `padding-bottom`, `padding-left`, or the `padding` shorthand). Padding takes on the background color of the element.

3. **Border Box:** This is the border line itself, sitting *between* the padding and the margin. You control its appearance with `border` properties (`border-width`, `border-style`, `border-color`, or the `border` shorthand).

4. **Margin Box:** This is the space *outside* the border. Margin pushes the element away from other elements around it. You control it with the `margin` properties (`margin-top`, `margin-right`, `margin-bottom`, `margin-left`, or the `margin` shorthand). Margin is always transparent.

Visualization:

```
+----------------------+
|      MARGIN          |
|   +---------------+  |
|   |    BORDER     |  |
|   |  +---------+  |  |
|   |  | PADDING |  |  |  <-- Takes background color
|   |  | +-----+ |  |  |
|   |  | |CONTENT| |  |  |  <-- Dimensions set by width/height
|   |  | +-----+ |  |  |
|   |  | PADDING |  |  |  <-- Takes background color
|   |  +---------+  |  |
|   |    BORDER     |  |
|   +---------------+  |
|      MARGIN          |  <-- Transparent
+----------------------+
```

Example:

```css
.my-box {
  width: 200px;       /* Content box width */
  height: 100px;      /* Content box height */
```

```
padding: 20px;      /* 20px padding on all four sides */
border: 5px solid blue; /* 5px blue border on all four sides */
margin: 15px;       /* 15px margin on all four sides */
background-color: lightcoral;
}
```
In the example above, an element with the class `.my-box` will visually occupy:

- **Width:** 200px (content) + 20px (left padding) + 20px (right padding) + 5px (left border) + 5px (right border) = **250px** total width.
- **Height:** 100px (content) + 20px (top padding) + 20px (bottom padding) + 5px (top border) + 5px (bottom border) = **150px** total height.

And then it will have 15px of transparent space (margin) around this 250x150px area, pushing it away from other elements.

The `box-sizing` Property:

By default, CSS uses the `content-box` model (this was the calculation above). This can be counter-intuitive because the `width` and `height` properties only control the *content* area, and padding and border *add* to the total size.

A more intuitive model for layout is often `border-box`. When `box-sizing: border-box;` is applied, the `width` and `height` properties include the padding and border. The content area *shrinks* to accommodate them.

```
.my-border-box {
  box-sizing: border-box; /* Change the box model */
  width: 200px;        /* Total width including padding and border */
  height: 100px;       /* Total height including padding and border */
  padding: 20px;       /* 20px padding */
  border: 5px solid blue; /* 5px blue border */
  margin: 15px;        /* 15px margin (still outside) */
  background-color: lightgreen;
}
```
Now, with `box-sizing: border-box;`:

- **Width:** The total width *is* the declared 200px. The content area will be 200px - 20px (left padding) - 20px (right padding) - 5px (left border) - 5px (right border) = **150px** wide.
- **Height:** The total height *is* the declared 100px. The content area will be 100px - 20px (top padding) - 20px (bottom padding) - 5px (top border) - 5px (bottom border) = **50px** tall.

Personal Insight: Setting `box-sizing: border-box;` globally for all elements is a very common practice in modern CSS development (`*, *::before, *::after { box-sizing: border-box; }`). It makes working with widths and heights much more predictable, especially when you add borders or padding to elements. I highly recommend adopting this habit early on!

Understanding the box model is crucial because it dictates how elements take up space on the page. It's fundamental to creating layouts with padding, borders, and margins.

1.5 Using CSS Comments and Organizing Your Styles

As you write more CSS, your files can quickly grow. Keeping them readable and organized is key to maintainability, especially when working on larger projects or collaborating with others. This is where comments and basic organization come in.

CSS Comments:

Comments are notes you add to your code that the browser completely ignores. They are there purely for human readers (including your future self!). In CSS, comments start with `/*` and end with `*/`. You can use them for single lines or multiple lines.

```css
/*
  This is a multi-line comment.
  It explains the purpose of the styles below.
*/


/* --- General Styles --- */

body {
  font-family: sans-serif; /* Set a basic font */
  line-height: 1.6; /* Improve readability */
  margin: 0; /* Remove default body margin */
}


/* --- Component: Button --- */
/* Styles specifically for interactive buttons */
.button {
  display: inline-block; /* Make button behave like a box but flow like text */
  padding: 10px 20px;
  background-color: #007bff;
  color: white;
  border: none;
```

```
  border-radius: 5px;
  cursor: pointer;
  text-decoration: none; /* Remove underline for link-buttons */
}


/* Modifier for a different button style */
.button-secondary {
  background-color: #6c757d;
}
```

- **Use comments to:**
    - Explain the purpose of a complex rule or section.
    - Divide your CSS into logical sections (see organization below).
    - Leave notes about why something was done a certain way.
    - Temporarily "comment out" code for debugging without deleting it.

Organizing Your Styles:

There's no single "right" way to organize CSS, but having *some* system is infinitely better than none. A few common approaches include:

- **By Element Type:** Group all h1, h2, p styles together, all button styles together, etc. (Can get messy with classes).
- **By Component/Module:** Group all styles related to a specific UI component (like a "card", "navigation bar", "modal") together. This is very popular in component-based frameworks like React.
- **By Function/Section:** Group styles by what they affect (e.g., "Typography", "Layout", "Colors", "Forms", "Utilities"). This is good for larger global stylesheets.
- **Alphabetical:** Sort properties within a rule alphabetically (e.g., border, color, font-size, margin, padding). This helps find properties quickly.

Using comments to clearly label sections, whichever organizational method you choose, is key.

Personal Insight: Trying to understand someone else's (or my own old!) CSS file with no comments or organization is like trying to navigate a city with no street signs. I've learned the hard way that spending a few extra moments adding comments and organizing code saves *hours* of confusion down the road. Find an organizational style that makes sense to you and stick with it!

Chapter 1 Summary

Phew! We covered some ground in this foundational chapter:

- You now know the basic syntax of a CSS rule: a **selector** targeting elements and a **declaration block** containing **declarations** (property: value;).

- You learned about the essential selector types: **Type**, **Class**, **ID**, and **Attribute** selectors, and how to use them to pick out specific HTML elements.
- You tackled the critical concepts of the **Cascade**, **Specificity** (the browser's tie-breaker), and **Inheritance** (how styles flow down the tree), which explain why certain styles apply.
- You understand that every element is a **Box**, and learned about the **Box Model**'s components: Content, Padding, Border, and Margin, and the difference between `content-box` and `border-box`.
- Finally, you saw the importance of **Comments** and basic **Organization** for keeping your CSS maintainable.

These are the absolute fundamentals. Everything else we do in CSS builds upon these concepts. Get comfortable with them, experiment in your browser's developer tools, and practice targeting elements and applying simple styles.

In the next chapter, we'll take this knowledge and apply it to creating actual layouts, starting with the more traditional methods before we jump into the modern world of Flexbox and Grid!

Chapter 2: Basic Layout and Positioning

You've got your HTML structure ready, and you know how to apply basic styles like colors, fonts, and borders using selectors. That's fantastic! But when you open your page, you might find elements just stacking up vertically or flowing in ways you don't expect. This is because browsers have default ways of displaying elements. To get beyond that, we need to learn how to explicitly control how boxes behave and where they sit on the page.

This chapter is all about gaining control over that "box" we talked about in Chapter 1 – not just styling its appearance, but defining its behavior and position relative to other boxes or the browser window itself.

2.1 Controlling Element Display: Block, Inline, Inline-Block, and None

The `display` property is one of the most fundamental in CSS when it comes to layout. It determines the *type* of box an element generates and how it interacts with other elements around it on the page. Every HTML element has a default `display` value (like `<div>` is block, `<span>` is inline), but you can override this with CSS.

Let's look at the most common values you'll encounter and use:

display: block;

- **Behavior:** A block-level element always starts on a new line and takes up the full width available within its parent container (unless you specify a width). Block elements stack vertically, one after the other.
- **Properties:** You can set `width`, `height`, `margin-top`, `margin-bottom`, `padding`, and `border` on block elements, and they will behave exactly as the Box Model described.
- **Examples of default block elements:** `<div>`, `<p>`, `<h1>` to `<h6>`, `<ul>`, `<li>`, `<form>`, `<header>`, `<footer>`, `<article>`, `<section>`.

```html
<!-- HTML -->
<div>This is a block div.</div>
<div>This is another block div. They stack.</div>
/* CSS */
div {
  background-color: lightblue;
  margin: 10px; /* Margin pushes them apart */
  padding: 5px;
}
```

(Result: Two blue boxes, each taking up the full width, with space above and below)

display: inline;

- **Behavior:** An inline element does *not* start on a new line. It only takes up as much width as its content requires and flows horizontally with surrounding text and inline elements.
- **Properties:** You *cannot* set `width` or `height` on inline elements – they are ignored. `margin-top` and `margin-bottom` are also ignored (though `margin-left` and `margin-right` work). `padding` and `border` *do* apply, but vertical padding/border might overlap content on the lines above or below.
- **Examples of default inline elements:** `<span>`, `<a>`, `<strong>`, `<em>`, `<img>`.

```
<!-- HTML -->
<span>This is an inline span.</span> <span>This is another. They flow
side-by-side.</span>
/* CSS */
span {
  background-color: lightgreen;
  margin: 10px; /* Only left/right margin works */
  padding: 10px; /* Padding works, but might overlap vertically */
}
```

(Result: Two green highlighted text spans next to each other. Vertical margins are ignored, vertical padding might cause overlap.)

`display: inline-block;`

- **Behavior:** This is a hybrid! An inline-block element flows horizontally with other inline and inline-block elements (like `inline`), but it *also* respects `width`, `height`, `margin`, and `padding` (like `block`). It's often used to create grid-like structures where items sit side-by-side but you need control over their dimensions and spacing.
- **Properties:** You can set `width`, `height`, and all margin/padding properties as you would on a block element.
- **Use case:** Creating horizontal lists (like navigation menus), arranging groups of images or cards in rows, or simply making an inline element behave more like a block element while keeping it in line.

```
<!-- HTML -->
<div style="background-color: #eee; padding: 10px;">
  <div class="inline-block-box">Box 1</div>
  <div class="inline-block-box">Box 2</div>
  <div class="inline-block-box">Box 3</div>
</div>
/* CSS */
.inline-block-box {
  display: inline-block; /* Key property */
  width: 100px;
```

```css
  height: 50px;
  background-color: lightcoral;
  margin: 10px; /* All margins work */
  padding: 5px;
}
```
(Result: Three light coral boxes, 100x50px each, sitting side-by-side within the gray container, with margins around them.)

Personal Insight: Back before Flexbox and Grid were widely supported or commonly used, `display: inline-block` was the go-to technique for creating responsive grid layouts. You'd set items to `inline-block`, give them a percentage width, and manage the spacing carefully. It worked, but it had quirks (like dealing with whitespace between elements in the HTML causing gaps). Flexbox and Grid are much more robust for complex grid systems now, but `inline-block` is still invaluable for specific scenarios where you need an element to behave inline but have block properties (like custom button styles that need padding and width).

display: none;

- **Behavior:** This completely hides the element. It's removed from the document flow, and it takes up *no space* on the page. It's as if the element wasn't even in the HTML.
- **Use case:** Hiding content that's not currently needed (e.g., modal windows before they're opened, content for different tabs). This is often toggled using JavaScript.

```css
/* CSS */
.hidden-element {
  display: none; /* Nobody sees me, I take no space! */
}
```
(Note: `visibility: hidden;` is different. It hides the element visually, but it still occupies space in the layout.)

Mastering `display` is your first step to controlling how elements interact with each other horizontally and vertically.

2.2 Understanding CSS Positioning: Static, Relative, Absolute, Fixed, Sticky

While `display` affects how elements interact in the normal flow, the `position` property allows you to take elements *out* of that flow or adjust their position based on different reference points. It works hand-in-hand with the `top`, `right`, `bottom`, and `left` offset properties, and the `z-index` property (which controls stacking order).

Let's explore the `position` values:

position: static;

- **Behavior:** This is the **default** value for every element. Elements are positioned according to the normal document flow.
- **Properties:** The `top`, `right`, `bottom`, `left`, and `z-index` properties have **NO effect** when `position` is `static`.

```css
/* CSS */
/* These divs will ignore top/left */
.static-box {
  position: static; /* This is the default anyway */
  background-color: lightblue;
  margin: 10px;
  top: 20px;    /* Ignored */
  left: 30px;   /* Ignored */
}
```
(Result: Boxes stack normally, ignoring the `top` and `left` values.)

position: relative;

- **Behavior:** An element with `position: relative;` is positioned according to the normal document flow, *then* offset from its normal position based on the `top`, `right`, `bottom`, and `left` values. Crucially, the space the element *would have occupied* in the normal flow is preserved – other elements don't move into that space.
- **Properties:** `top`, `right`, `bottom`, `left` *do* work, shifting the element *relative to itself*. `z-index` *does* work to control stacking order relative to other positioned elements.
- **Key secondary use:** `position: relative;` makes the element a **positioning context** for any absolutely positioned children it contains.

```css
/* CSS */
.relative-box {
  position: relative;
  background-color: lightgreen;
  width: 200px;
  height: 100px;
  margin: 20px;
  top: 30px; /* Shifted 30px down from its normal position */
  left: 50px; /* Shifted 50px right from its normal position */
}


.another-box {
  background-color: lightblue;
```

```
  width: 200px;
  height: 100px;
  margin: 20px;
}
```

(Result: The green box is shifted down and right, potentially overlapping the blue box. The space where the green box would have been is still empty in the layout.)

position: absolute;

- **Behavior:** An element with `position: absolute;` is removed entirely from the normal document flow. It doesn't affect the position of surrounding elements, and they act as if it's not there. The element is positioned relative to its *nearest positioned ancestor* (an ancestor with `position` set to `relative`, `absolute`, `fixed`, or `sticky`). If there is no positioned ancestor, it's positioned relative to the initial containing block (often the `<html>` element).
- **Properties:** `top`, `right`, `bottom`, `left` work relative to the *edge of its positioning context*. `z-index` controls stacking order.
- **Use case:** Placing elements on top of others, like badges on an icon, close buttons on modals, or tooltips.

```html
<!-- HTML -->
<div class="container-relative">
  <div class="box-absolute">Badge</div>
  <img src="some-icon.png" alt="Icon">
</div>
```

```css
/* CSS */
.container-relative {
  position: relative; /* This makes it the positioning context */
  display: inline-block; /* So it doesn't take full width */
  border: 1px solid black;
  padding: 10px;
}

.box-absolute {
  position: absolute; /* Positioned relative to .container-relative */
  top: -10px; /* 10px up from the top edge of .container-relative */
  right: -10px; /* 10px left from the right edge of .container-
relative */
  background-color: red;
  color: white;
  padding: 5px;
```

```
  border-radius: 3px;
  font-size: 0.8em;
}
```

(Result: The "Badge" box is positioned at the top-right corner outside the border of the black container, overlapping surrounding content if any exists.)

Personal Insight: Debugging `position: absolute;` is often a matter of figuring out *what* element is its positioning context. If your absolutely positioned element seems to be positioning itself relative to the whole page instead of its parent, nine times out of ten it's because the parent (or nearest ancestor you *thought* was the context) doesn't have a `position` property set to anything other than `static`. Setting `position: relative;` on the parent is a common pattern for this reason.

position: fixed;

- **Behavior:** An element with `position: fixed;` is removed from the normal document flow and positioned relative to the **viewport** (the browser window). It stays in that exact position even when the page is scrolled.
- **Properties:** `top, right, bottom, left` work relative to the edges of the *viewport*. `z-index` controls stacking order relative to other elements.
- **Use case:** Creating sticky headers or footers that are always visible, "scroll-to-top" buttons, or persistent sidebars.

```html
<!-- HTML -->
<body>
  <div class="fixed-header">Site Title</div>
  <!-- Plenty of content here to make the page scroll -->
  <div style="height: 2000px;">Scroll down!</div>
</body>
/* CSS */
.fixed-header {
  position: fixed; /* Stays fixed in the viewport */
  top: 0; /* Aligned to the top edge of the viewport */
  left: 0; /* Aligned to the left edge of the viewport */
  width: 100%; /* Takes full width of the viewport */
  background-color: #f1f1f1;
  padding: 10px;
  text-align: center;
  z-index: 1000; /* Ensure it's above most other content */
}
```

```css
/* Add padding to body to prevent content from being hidden under the
fixed header */
body {
  padding-top: 40px; /* Adjust based on header height */
}
```
(Result: The gray header remains at the top of the browser window as you scroll the content below it.)

position: sticky;

- **Behavior:** This is a bit of a hybrid. An element with `position: sticky;` behaves like `position: relative;` within its parent container until its position crosses a specified threshold (`top`, `right`, `bottom`, or `left` is required for the stickiness to activate). At that point, it becomes 'stuck' like a `position: fixed;` element relative to the viewport, until its parent container scrolls out of view.
- **Properties:** Requires at least one of `top`, `right`, `bottom`, or `left` to define the sticky offset. `z-index` works.
- **Use case:** Sticky table headers, section headers that stay visible while you scroll through the section's content, sticky sidebars that scroll for a while then stop at a certain point.

```html
<!-- HTML -->
<div class="sticky-container">
  <div class="sticky-header">Section Header</div>
  <p>Content...</p>
  <p>Content...</p>
  <!-- More content -->
</div>
<!-- More content outside the container -->
<div style="height: 1000px; background-color: lightblue;">More content
below...</div>
```
```css
/* CSS */
.sticky-container {
  /* Height required for sticky element to scroll within it */
  height: 300px;
  overflow-y: scroll; /* Needed for the sticky element to scroll with
content */
  border: 1px solid gray;
}

.sticky-header {
```

```
  position: sticky;
  top: 0; /* This is the key: it sticks when it hits the top of the
container/viewport */
  background-color: #ffebcc;
  padding: 10px;
  text-align: center;
}
```

(Result: As you scroll the container, the "Section Header" initially scrolls normally, but once it reaches the top edge of the container's visible area, it stays fixed there until the entire container has scrolled out of view.)

2.3 Managing Content Overflow

What happens when the content inside a box is larger than the box's dimensions? By default, the content simply spills out, or "overflows." The `overflow` property controls this behavior.

It's most commonly applied to block-level elements or elements with a defined `height` or `max-height`.

- **`overflow: visible;`:** (Default) Content overflows the element's box.
- **`overflow: hidden;`:** Content is clipped at the element's edge and the overflowing part is invisible.
- **`overflow: scroll;`:** Scrollbars are *always* added to the element, allowing the user to scroll through the content, even if it doesn't currently overflow.
- **`overflow: auto;`:** Scrollbars are added *only if* the content overflows. This is often the most practical choice as it only introduces scrollbars when necessary.

You can also control overflow on individual axes using `overflow-x` (horizontal) and `overflow-y` (vertical).

```
/* CSS */
.overflow-box {
  width: 200px;
  height: 100px;
  border: 1px solid black;
  /* Try changing this overflow value */
  overflow: auto; /* Or visible, hidden, scroll */
}
<!-- HTML -->
<div class="overflow-box">
```

```
<p>This paragraph has content that might be longer than the box.
Let's add more text to make sure it definitely overflows vertically to
test the overflow property. Hopefully, this is enough text!</p>
</div>
```
(Result: With `overflow: auto;`*, scrollbars will appear on the box if the paragraph's text exceeds the box's height. With* `visible`*, the text spills out. With* `hidden`*, it's cut off. With* `scroll`*, scrollbars are always there.)*

2.4 Practical Use Cases for Basic Layout Techniques

So, while Flexbox and Grid are your heavy lifters for overall page structure and component arrangements, these basic techniques are still vital:

- **Inline-Block:** Use it when you need elements to sit side-by-side but require control over their width/height and margins (e.g., a list of circular avatars, small icons with labels next to them).
- **Relative Positioning:** Great for making minor adjustments to an element's position without affecting the flow, or critically, for establishing a positioning context for absolutely positioned children.
- **Absolute Positioning:** Essential for overlaying elements precisely on top of others (badges, tooltips, dropdown menus opening from a button). Remember the `position: relative;` parent pattern!
- **Fixed Positioning:** Your go-to for persistent elements that must stay visible in the viewport (headers, footers, chat widgets).
- **Sticky Positioning:** Perfect for elements that need to scroll normally for a while then latch onto a screen edge (sticky headers in long lists, navigation sections).
- **Overflow:** Crucial for controlling content in fixed-size containers, preventing unwanted spillage, or explicitly creating scrollable regions within a page section (e.g., a scrollable terms and conditions box, a code snippet container).

Don't dismiss these basic techniques! They solve specific problems elegantly and efficiently. Think of them as precision tools for individual elements or small groups, complementing the broader layout power of Flexbox and Grid.

Chapter 2 Summary

We've added some powerful tools to our CSS layout kit:

- You understand the `display` property and the difference between `block`, `inline`, `inline-block`, and `none`, and how they affect an element's flow and dimensions.
- You've learned about the `position` property and its key values: `static`, `relative`, `absolute`, `fixed`, and `sticky`, and how they determine an element's reference point for positioning.
- You know how `top`, `right`, `bottom`, `left`, and `z-index` work with positioned elements.
- You explored the `overflow` property (`visible`, `hidden`, `scroll`, `auto`) to control content that exceeds its container's bounds.
- You saw practical examples of how these techniques are used in real-world scenarios.

You can now control whether an element takes up a full line or flows horizontally, and how it's positioned relative to its normal spot, its parent, or the viewport. This is a huge step! Practice playing with `display` and `position` on simple boxes in your code editor and inspect them in the browser developer tools to see how they affect the layout.

Ready to tackle more flexible and powerful layout challenges? In the next chapter, we dive into Flexbox, which revolutionized how we build one-dimensional layouts like navigation bars and component rows!

Chapter 3: Flexbox: The Flexible Layout Module

Welcome to Flexbox! This is a CSS layout module that provides a more efficient way to arrange, align, and distribute space among items in a container, even when their size is unknown or dynamic. The main idea behind Flexbox is to give the container the ability to alter its items' width/height (and order) to best fill the available space.

The key concept to grasp upfront is that **Flexbox is designed for one-dimensional layout**. This means you arrange items primarily along a single axis at a time – either a row *or* a column. If you need to lay things out in both rows *and* columns simultaneously (like a spreadsheet or a complex dashboard grid), you'll likely reach for CSS Grid (which we'll cover next). But for laying out items in a line, a row of buttons, a navigation bar, or even a simple form, Flexbox is often the perfect tool.

3.1 Introduction to Flexbox Concepts and Terminology

To work with Flexbox, you need to understand a few core terms. It revolves around two main elements:

1. **The Flex Container:** This is the parent element you apply `display: flex;` (or `display: inline-flex;`) to. Once an element becomes a flex container, its *direct children* become flex items.
2. **The Flex Items:** These are the direct children of the flex container. They are the elements that will be laid out according to the Flexbox rules you set on their parent.

These elements interact based on two axes:

- **Main Axis:** This is the primary axis along which flex items are laid out. By default, it's a horizontal axis running from left to right.
- **Cross Axis:** This axis is perpendicular to the main axis. By default (when the main axis is horizontal), the cross axis is vertical, running from top to bottom.

You can change the direction of the main axis, which in turn changes the direction of the cross axis.

- **Main Start/End:** The beginning and end of the main axis.
- **Cross Start/End:** The beginning and end of the cross axis.
- **Main Size:** A flex item's width or height, depending on the main axis direction.
- **Cross Size:** A flex item's width or height, depending on the cross axis direction.

It might sound a bit abstract, but once you see it visually, it clicks.

Imagine the container is a road. The `main-axis` is the direction the cars (flex items) are driving. The `cross-axis` is perpendicular to the road – think of parking spots or buildings lining the road.

```
<!-- HTML -->
```

```
<div class="flex-container">
  <div class="flex-item">1</div>
  <div class="flex-item">2</div>
  <div class="flex-item">3</div>
</div>
/* CSS */
.flex-container {
  /* This turns the div into a flex container */
  display: flex;
  /* Basic styling to see the container and items */
  border: 2px solid blue;
  padding: 10px;
  min-height: 150px; /* Give it some height so alignment is visible */
}


.flex-item {
  background-color: lightgray;
  border: 1px solid black;
  padding: 10px;
  margin: 5px;
}
```
In this default scenario:

- `.flex-container` is the flex container.
- The three `.flex-item` divs are the flex items.
- The main axis is horizontal (default `flex-direction: row;`).
- The cross axis is vertical.
- Items are laid out side-by-side from the Main Start (left) to the Main End (right).

3.2 Arranging Items with Flex Container Properties (flex-direction, flex-wrap)

These properties are set on the **flex container** and determine the overall arrangement of its items.

display: flex; or display: inline-flex;

- This is the magic switch! Apply this to a parent element, and its direct children become flex items.
- `display: flex;` makes the flex container itself a block-level element (takes full width, starts on new line).

- `display: inline-flex;` makes the flex container itself an inline-level element (flows with surrounding content, only takes content width).
- *Most of the time, you'll use* `display: flex;`.

flex-direction

- Controls the direction of the **main axis**.
- Values:
  - `row` (default): Main axis is horizontal (left to right in LTR languages).
  - `row-reverse`: Main axis is horizontal, but starts from the end (right to left).
  - `column`: Main axis is vertical (top to bottom).
  - `column-reverse`: Main axis is vertical, but starts from the end (bottom to top).

Example:

```
.container-row {
  display: flex;
  flex-direction: row; /* Default, items go left to right */
  border: 1px solid red;
}


.container-column {
  display: flex;
  flex-direction: column; /* Items go top to bottom */
  border: 1px solid green;
  height: 200px; /* Need height to see column layout clearly */
}


.item {
  padding: 10px;
  border: 1px solid black;
  background-color: #eee;
  margin: 5px;
}


<!-- HTML -->
<div class="container-row">
  <div class="item">1</div>
  <div class="item">2</div>
  <div class="item">3</div>
</div>
```

```
<div class="container-column">
  <div class="item">A</div>
  <div class="item">B</div>
  <div class="item">C</div>
</div>
```

(Result: Top container shows items 1, 2, 3 horizontally. Bottom container shows items A, B, C vertically.)

flex-wrap

- Controls whether flex items are forced onto a single line or can wrap onto multiple lines when the container isn't wide/tall enough to hold them all.
- Values:
  - `nowrap` (default): Items will shrink to fit or overflow the container, staying on one line.
  - `wrap`: Items will wrap onto new lines if needed. New lines are added below the previous line (for `row`) or to the right (for `column`).
  - `wrap-reverse`: Items will wrap onto new lines, but the new lines appear *above* the previous line (for `row`) or to the left (for `column`).

Example:

```
.container-wrap {
  display: flex;
  flex-wrap: wrap; /* Items will wrap if container is too narrow */
  width: 200px; /* Make container narrow to force wrapping */
  border: 1px solid purple;
}

.item-wide {
  width: 80px; /* Give items width so they take up space */
  height: 50px;
  background-color: orange;
  margin: 5px;
}

<!-- HTML -->
<div class="container-wrap">
```

```
<div class="item-wide">1</div>
<div class="item-wide">2</div>
<div class="item-wide">3</div>
<div class="item-wide">4</div>
<div class="item-wide">5</div>
</div>
```

content_copydownload

Use code with caution.Html

(Result: Items 1 and 2 might fit on the first line, then 3 and 4 wrap to the next line below, and 5 wraps to a third line below that, because the container is only 200px wide and items are 80px + margins.)

`flex-flow` (Shorthand)

- Shorthand for `flex-direction` and `flex-wrap`.
- Syntax: `flex-flow: <direction> <wrap>;`
- Example: `flex-flow: row wrap;` is the same as `flex-direction: row;` and `flex-wrap: wrap;`.

Personal Insight: I almost always set `flex-wrap: wrap;` when building components like card grids or lists of tags. Forgetting `flex-wrap` on a horizontal flex container means items will just aggressively shrink or overflow off the screen on narrow views, which is rarely what you want for responsive design. Always consider if your items should wrap!

3.3 Aligning Items Along the Main and Cross Axis (`justify-content, align-items, align-content`)

These properties control how space is distributed and how items are aligned within the flex container. This is where much of the layout magic happens!

`justify-content`

- Aligns flex items *along the **main axis***. It distributes extra space or handles overflow along this axis.
- Values:
  - `flex-start` (default for `row`): Items are packed towards the start of the main axis.
  - `flex-end`: Items are packed towards the end of the main axis.
  - `center`: Items are centered along the main axis.
  - `space-between`: Items are evenly distributed; the first item is at the start, the last is at the end. Space is put *between* items.

o `space-around`: Items are evenly distributed with equal space around them. The space *before* the first item and *after* the last item is half the space between items.
o `space-evenly`: Items are distributed so that the space between any two items (and the space to the edges) is equal.

Example (assuming `flex-direction: row;`):

```css
.container-justify {
  display: flex;
  justify-content: center; /* Try changing to flex-start, flex-end,
space-between, space-around, space-evenly */
  border: 1px solid blue;
  height: 80px; /* Give space to see alignment */
}

.item-small {
  width: 50px;
  background-color: lightgray;
  border: 1px solid black;
}
```

```html
<!-- HTML -->
<div class="container-justify">
  <div class="item-small">1</div>
  <div class="item-small">2</div>
  <div class="item-small">3</div>
</div>
```

(Result: With `justify-content: center;`, the three small boxes will be grouped together in the horizontal center of the blue container.)

align-items

- Aligns flex items *along the **cross axis*** within *each line*. It determines their alignment perpendicular to the main axis.
- Values:
    o `stretch` (default): Flex items stretch to fill the container's cross-axis size (but respect `max-height`/`max-width`).
    o `flex-start`: Items are packed towards the start of the cross axis.
    o `flex-end`: Items are packed towards the end of the cross axis.

- center: Items are centered along the cross axis.
- baseline: Items are aligned based on their baselines (the line the text sits on).

Example (assuming `flex-direction: row;`*):*

```css
.container-align-items {
  display: flex;
  align-items: center; /* Try changing to stretch, flex-start, flex-
end, baseline */
  border: 1px solid green;
  height: 100px; /* Essential to see alignment along cross axis */
}

.item {
  width: 50px;
  padding: 5px;
  border: 1px solid black;
  background-color: #eee;
  /* Remove margin-top/bottom if present from previous examples, as
align-items affects position */
  margin: 0 5px;
}

.item-tall {
  height: 80px; /* Make one item taller to see stretching/alignment */
}
```

```html
<!-- HTML -->
<div class="container-align-items">
  <div class="item">Short</div>
  <div class="item item-tall">Tall</div>
  <div class="item">Short</div>
</div>
```

(Result: With `align-items: center;`*, all items will be vertically centered within the 100px tall green container, regardless of their individual height.)*

Personal Insight: `justify-content: center;` and `align-items: center;` are the magical duo for perfectly centering a single item or a group of items within a container using

Flexbox. Forget the old tricks with `margin: auto` or `position: absolute;` with transforms – this is the modern, clean way.

`align-content`

- Aligns the *lines* of flex items *along the **cross axis*** when there is *extra space in the cross axis* and `flex-wrap` is set to `wrap`. This property only has an effect if you have multiple lines of flex items.
- Values: Similar to `justify-content` - `flex-start`, `flex-end`, `center`, `space-between`, `space-around`, `stretch` (default).

Example (requires `flex-wrap: wrap;` and sufficient height):

```css
.container-align-content {
  display: flex;
  flex-wrap: wrap;
  height: 300px; /* Plenty of extra space in the cross axis */
  border: 1px solid purple;
  align-content: space-around; /* Try changing to stretch, flex-start,
center, etc. */
}


.item-wide {
  width: 80px;
  height: 50px;
  background-color: orange;
  margin: 5px;
}
```

```html
<!-- HTML -->
<div class="container-align-content">
  <div class="item-wide">1</div>
  <div class="item-wide">2</div>
  <div class="item-wide">3</div>
  <div class="item-wide">4</div>
  <div class="item-wide">5</div>
  <div class="item-wide">6</div>
  <div class="item-wide">7</div>
  <div class="item-wide">8</div>
</div>
```

(Result: If the items wrap onto multiple lines, `align-content: space-around;` will distribute the extra 200px+ height in the container by putting even space around each horizontal line of items.)

3.4 Controlling Flex Items Individually (flex-grow, flex-shrink, flex-basis, `align-self`, `order`)

These properties are applied directly to the **flex items** (the children of the container) to override or customize their behavior within the flex layout.

order

- Controls the **visual order** of a flex item within the flex container. By default, items appear in the source order (`order: 0;`). You can assign integer values (positive or negative) to change their display order. Items with lower `order` values appear before items with higher values.
- *Important:* `order` only changes the *visual* order, not the order in the HTML source code. This can impact accessibility and SEO, so use it judiciously.

Example:

```css
.container {
  display: flex;
}

.item {
  padding: 10px;
  border: 1px solid black;
  margin: 5px;
}

.item-a { background-color: lightblue; order: 2; }
.item-b { background-color: lightgreen; order: 1; }
.item-c { background-color: lightcoral; order: 3; }
```

```html
<!-- HTML -->
<div class="container">
  <div class="item item-a">A</div>
  <div class="item item-b">B</div>
  <div class="item item-c">C</div>
</div>
```

(Result: Even though the HTML source is A, B, C, the visual order will be B, A, C because of the `order` values.)

flex-grow

- Specifies how much a flex item will grow relative to the rest of the flex items in the container when there's extra space on the main axis.
- Takes a unitless number as a value (e.g., 1, 2).
- Default is 0 (item does not grow).
- If all items have flex-grow: 1;, they will all grow equally to fill the available space. If one has flex-grow: 2; and another flex-grow: 1;, the item with 2 will take up twice as much of the extra space as the item with 1.

Example:

```css
.container {
  display: flex;
  width: 400px; /* Container wider than items combined */
  border: 1px solid blue;
}


.item {
  width: 80px; /* Base width */
  height: 50px;
  background-color: lightgray;
  margin: 5px;
}


.item-grow {
  flex-grow: 1; /* This item will grow */
  background-color: lightgreen;
}


<!-- HTML -->
<div class="container">
  <div class="item">1</div>
  <div class="item item-grow">2 (Grows)</div>
  <div class="item">3</div>
</div>
```

(Result: Items 1 and 3 stay at 80px width (+margins). Item 2 expands to fill all the remaining horizontal space in the container.)

flex-shrink

- Specifies how much a flex item will shrink relative to the rest of the flex items when there's not enough space on the main axis (i.e., when items would overflow).
- Takes a unitless number (e.g., `1`, `0`).
- Default is `1` (item can shrink).
- Setting `flex-shrink: 0;` prevents an item from shrinking below its `flex-basis` or content size.

Example:

```css
.container {
  display: flex;
  width: 200px; /* Container narrower than items combined */
  border: 1px solid red;
}


.item {
  width: 80px; /* Base width - these items WANT to be 80px */
  height: 50px;
  background-color: lightgray;
  margin: 5px;
}


.item-no-shrink {
  flex-shrink: 0; /* This item will NOT shrink below 80px */
  background-color: lightcoral;
}
```
```html
<!-- HTML -->
<div class="container">
  <div class="item">1</div>
  <div class="item item-no-shrink">2 (No Shrink)</div>
  <div class="item">3</div>
</div>
```

(Result: Items 1 and 3 will shrink to fit within the 200px container. Item 2 will attempt to stay at 80px, likely causing the items to overflow the container because it refused to shrink.)

flex-basis

- Specifies the initial size of a flex item *before* extra space is distributed or items shrink. It's the starting point for `flex-grow` and `flex-shrink`.

- Can be a length (e.g., `100px`, `50%`, `5em`) or `auto` (default - the item's size is based on its content or its `width`/`height` property if set).
- If `flex-basis` is set to a non-`auto` value, it overrides the item's `width` (if `flex-direction: row;`) or `height` (if `flex-direction: column;`).

Example:

```
.container {
  display: flex;
  width: 300px;
  border: 1px solid green;
}


.item {
  height: 50px;
  background-color: #eee;
  margin: 5px;
  flex-grow: 1; /* All items grow equally */
}


.item-basis {
  flex-basis: 100px; /* This item's starting size is 100px */
  background-color: lightblue;
}


<!-- HTML -->
<div class="container">
  <div class="item">1</div>
  <div class="item item-basis">2 (Basis 100px)</div>
  <div class="item">3</div>
</div>
```

(Result: Item 2 starts at 100px. Items 1 and 3 have `flex-basis: auto;` (or effectively based on content/default width if no width set). All items then grow to fill the remaining space based on their `flex-grow: 1;` value, but because item 2 started larger, it will end up larger than 1 and 3.)

flex (Shorthand)

- Shorthand for `flex-grow`, `flex-shrink`, and `flex-basis`.

- Syntax: `flex: <grow> <shrink> <basis>;`
- Example: `flex: 1 1 auto;` (Equivalent of `flex-grow: 1; flex-shrink: 1; flex-basis: auto;`)
- Common values:
  - `flex: auto;` (Equivalent of `flex: 1 1 auto;`) - Item grows, shrinks, and basis is `auto`.
  - `flex: none;` (Equivalent of `flex: 0 0 auto;`) - Item doesn't grow or shrink, basis is `auto`.
  - `flex: 0;` (Equivalent of `flex: 0 1 0%;`) - Item doesn't grow, can shrink, basis is 0. Use with caution.
  - `flex: 1;` (Equivalent of `flex: 1 1 0%;`) - Item grows, can shrink, basis is 0. This is very common for making items take up equal space.

Personal Insight: While it's good to understand the individual properties, you'll often see and use the `flex` shorthand in practice. `flex: 1;` is one of the most common Flexbox declarations – it tells an item to just "take up the available space" while being able to shrink if needed.

align-self

- Allows you to override the `align-items` property set on the flex container for a *single* flex item.
- Takes the same values as `align-items: auto` (default - inherits container's `align-items`), `stretch`, `flex-start`, `flex-end`, `center`, `baseline`.

Example:

```css
.container {
  display: flex;
  align-items: flex-start; /* All items align to the top by default */
  height: 150px;
  border: 1px solid blue;
}

.item {
  width: 50px;
  height: 60px;
  background-color: lightgray;
  border: 1px solid black;
  margin: 5px;
}

.item-center {
```

```
    align-self: center; /* This item will be centered vertically,
overriding container */
    background-color: lightgreen;
}


<!-- HTML -->
<div class="container">
  <div class="item">Top</div>
  <div class="item item-center">Center</div>
  <div class="item">Top</div>
</div>
```

(Result: The first and third items align to the top of the container, while the middle item is vertically centered within the container.)

3.5 Building Common Layouts with Flexbox

Now let's combine these properties to build some real-world layout patterns!

Centering Content (Horizontal & Vertical)

The classic problem solved easily with Flexbox.

```
<!-- HTML -->
<div class="center-container">
  <div class="centered-box">I am centered!</div>
</div>

/* CSS */
.center-container {
  display: flex;
  justify-content: center; /* Centers content horizontally */
  align-items: center; /* Centers content vertically */
  height: 200px; /* Give the container a height to see vertical
centering */
  border: 2px solid blue;
}


.centered-box {
  background-color: lightblue;
  padding: 20px;
```

```
}
```

(Result: The light blue box is perfectly centered within the blue container.)

Creating a Navigation Bar

A common use case: a row of links.

```html
<!-- HTML -->
<nav class="navbar">
  <a href="#" class="nav-link">Home</a>
  <a href="#" class="nav-link">About</a>
  <a href="#" class="nav-link">Services</a>
  <a href="#" class="nav-link">Contact</a>
</nav>
```

```css
/* CSS */
.navbar {
  display: flex; /* Arrange children (links) in a flex row */
  justify-content: space-around; /* Evenly distribute links */
  align-items: center; /* Vertically center links if navbar has
height/padding */
  background-color: #f8f8f8;
  padding: 10px 0;
  border-bottom: 1px solid #eee;
}

.nav-link {
  text-decoration: none;
  color: #333;
  padding: 5px 10px;
}

.nav-link:hover {
  color: blue;
}
```

(Result: A horizontal navigation bar with links spaced evenly along the row.)

Building a Simple Card Grid (Wrapping)

Using `flex-wrap` to create rows of items that automatically flow to the next line.

```html
<!-- HTML -->
<div class="card-grid-container">
  <div class="card">Card 1</div>
  <div class="card">Card 2</div>
  <div class="card">Card 3</div>
  <div class="card">Card 4</div>
  <div class="card">Card 5</div>
</div>
```

```css
/* CSS */
.card-grid-container {
  display: flex;
  flex-wrap: wrap; /* Items will wrap to the next line */
  justify-content: space-around; /* Optional: space out cards on each line */
  padding: 10px;
  border: 1px solid green;
}

.card {
  width: 150px; /* Give cards a base width */
  height: 100px;
  background-color: lightgreen;
  border: 1px solid darkgreen;
  margin: 10px; /* Margin creates space between cards */
  display: flex; /* Optional: Use flexbox inside the card to center its content */
  justify-content: center;
  align-items: center;
}
```

(Result: Cards will arrange themselves in rows. If the container isn't wide enough for all 5, they will wrap neatly onto subsequent lines.)

Sticky Footer using flex-grow

A common layout where the footer stays at the bottom, even if the content is short. The body/main container becomes a flex column.

```html
<!-- HTML -->
<body class="sticky-footer-body">
  <header class="sticky-header">Site Header</header>
  <main class="sticky-main-content">
    <h1>Main Content</h1>
    <p>Some content here. If there's not much content, we still want
the footer at the bottom.</p>
    <!-- Add more <p> tags or content if needed to test when main
content is taller -->
  </main>
  <footer class="sticky-footer">Site Footer</footer>
</body>
```

```css
/* CSS */
/* Reset default body margin/padding */
body {
  margin: 0;
  padding: 0;
}

.sticky-footer-body {
  display: flex;
  flex-direction: column; /* Stack children vertically */
  min-height: 100vh; /* Make the body at least viewport height */
}

.sticky-header, .sticky-footer {
  background-color: #f1f1f1;
  padding: 10px;
  text-align: center;
}

.sticky-main-content {
  flex-grow: 1; /* This is key: it takes up all available space */
  padding: 20px;
  /* Optional: add a background to see its area */
```

```
background-color: #fff;
}
```

(Result: The header is at the top, the footer is at the bottom. The `sticky-main-content` expands to push the footer down, ensuring it's always at the very bottom of the viewport if content is short, or after the content if content is long and makes the body taller than the viewport.)

Chapter 3 Summary

Flexbox is a game-changer for one-dimensional layouts. You now know:

- The core concepts: **Flex Container**, **Flex Items**, **Main Axis**, and **Cross Axis**.
- How to turn an element into a flex container using `display: flex;`.
- How to control the direction of the main axis with `flex-direction` (`row`, `column`, etc.).
- How to make items wrap onto new lines with `flex-wrap`.
- How to distribute space and align items along the main axis using `justify-content`.
- How to align items along the cross axis within their line using `align-items`.
- How to align multiple lines of items along the cross axis using `align-content` (when wrapping).
- How to control individual items with `order`, `flex-grow`, `flex-shrink`, `flex-basis`, and `align-self`.
- You've seen examples of common Flexbox layouts like centering, navigation bars, wrapping grids, and sticky footers.

Flexbox might feel like a lot to remember at first, but the key is to practice and understand the difference between properties on the *container* and properties on the *items*. The more you build with it, the more intuitive it becomes. Play with the code examples, change the values, and see how the layout changes. Use your browser's developer tools to inspect flex containers and items – browsers often have visual overlays that show the flex axes and spacing, which is incredibly helpful for learning.

Chapter 4: CSS Grid Layout: Creating Two-Dimensional Structures

You've mastered the CSS Box Model and basic positioning, and you've seen how Flexbox helps you arrange items along a single axis. Now, get ready for CSS Grid Layout. This module fundamentally changed how we build complex web layouts. Instead of hacking together columns with floats or wrestling with `inline-block`, Grid gives you a dedicated, powerful system for creating grid structures on your page.

While Flexbox is perfect for components like a row of buttons or items in a list, **CSS Grid is designed for laying out major page regions or groups of content in a two-dimensional grid.** Think headers, footers, sidebars, main content areas, or complex dashboards where items need to align both horizontally and vertically.

4.1 Introduction to CSS Grid: Rows, Columns, Cells, and Areas

Just like Flexbox, Grid introduces its own set of terms and concepts centered around a parent container and its direct children:

1. **Grid Container:** The element you apply `display: grid;` (or `display: inline-grid;`) to. Its direct children become Grid Items.
2. **Grid Items:** The direct children of the Grid Container. These are the elements you will place within the grid structure.
3. **Grid Lines:** The horizontal and vertical lines that define the grid structure. They are numbered starting from 1 at the top and left edges of the grid. You can also name these lines.
4. **Grid Tracks:** The spaces between two adjacent grid lines. These are your **Rows** (horizontal tracks) and **Columns** (vertical tracks). You define the size of these tracks.
5. **Grid Cells:** The smallest unit of a grid, formed by the intersection of a row track and a column track. It's like a single cell in a spreadsheet.
6. **Grid Areas:** A rectangular space encompassing one or more grid cells. You can define and name these areas to place grid items into them.

Visualizing the Grid:

Imagine a tic-tac-toe board.

- The board itself is the **Grid Container**.
- The lines separating the squares are the **Grid Lines** (4 lines total, 2 vertical, 2 horizontal).
- The horizontal spaces between the lines are the **Rows** (3 rows).
- The vertical spaces between the lines are the **Columns** (3 columns).
- Each individual square is a **Grid Cell**.
- You could define an **Area** that covers the entire top row, or the center square.

```html
<!-- HTML -->
<div class="grid-container">
  <div class="grid-item">1</div>
  <div class="grid-item">2</div>
  <div class="grid-item">3</div>
  <div class="grid-item">4</div>
  <div class="grid-item">5</div>
  <div class="grid-item">6</div>
</div>
```

```css
/* CSS */
.grid-container {
  /* This makes the div a grid container */
  display: grid;

  /* Define 3 columns, each 100px wide */
  grid-template-columns: 100px 100px 100px;

  /* Define 2 rows, each 50px tall */
  grid-template-rows: 50px 50px;

  /* Add some space between the grid cells */
  gap: 10px; /* Shorthand for grid-row-gap and grid-column-gap */

  /* Basic styling */
  border: 2px solid blue;
  padding: 10px;
}

.grid-item {
  background-color: lightgray;
  border: 1px solid black;
  padding: 5px;
  text-align: center;
}
```

In this basic example:

- `.grid-container` is the grid container.
- The six `.grid-item` divs are the grid items.
- `grid-template-columns: 100px 100px 100px;` creates 3 vertical tracks (columns).
- `grid-template-rows: 50px 50px;` creates 2 horizontal tracks (rows).
- This creates a 3x2 grid (6 cells).
- `gap: 10px;` puts 10px of space between grid cells, both horizontally and vertically.
- By default, the grid items are automatically placed into the grid cells, filling them row by row (item 1 in cell 1, item 2 in cell 2, etc.).

4.2 Defining Grid Structure with Container Properties (grid-template-`rows`, `grid-template-columns`, `grid-gap`)

These properties are set on the **Grid Container** to define the structure of your grid.

`display: grid;` or `display: inline-grid;`

- Activates Grid Layout for the direct children.
- `display: grid;` makes the container a block-level element.
- `display: inline-grid;` makes the container an inline-level element.
- *You'll primarily use `display: grid;`.*

`grid-template-columns` and `grid-template-rows`

- These are the heart of defining your grid structure. You list the sizes of the tracks you want to create.
- Values can be:
  - **Fixed Units:** px, em, rem, vw, vh, etc. (`grid-template-columns: 100px 200px auto;`)
  - **Percentages:** Relative to the grid container's size (`grid-template-columns: 25% 50% 25%;`)
  - **The `fr` Unit: A fractional unit.** `1fr` represents 1 portion of the available space in the grid container. This is incredibly useful for responsive layouts! (`grid-template-columns: 1fr 2fr 1fr;` would create three columns, the middle one being twice as wide as the other two, sharing the available space).
  - **`auto`:** The browser calculates the size based on the content or remaining space.
  - **`min-content` / `max-content`:** Sizes the track based on the minimum/maximum size the content needs.
  - **`minmax(min, max)`:** Creates a size range. The track will be *at least* min and *at most* max. Example: `minmax(100px, 1fr)` means the

column will be at least 100px, but can grow to take up 1 fraction of the space if more is available.

Example defining tracks:

```css
.my-layout {
  display: grid;
  /*
    Create 3 columns:
    - Auto-sized first column
    - Second column takes 1 fraction of available space
    - Third column is fixed at 150px
  */
  grid-template-columns: auto 1fr 150px;

  /*
    Create 2 rows:
    - First row is 80px tall
    - Second row is at least 100px, but can grow to take 1 fraction of
available space
  */
  grid-template-rows: 80px minmax(100px, 1fr);

  border: 2px solid purple;
  height: 300px; /* Give container height to see fr unit work */
}

.my-layout > div { /* Style direct children (items) */
  background-color: #eee;
  border: 1px solid #ccc;
  padding: 10px;
  text-align: center;
}
```

(Result: A grid with specific column and row sizes based on fixed units, auto, fr, and minmax. The `fr` unit in the second column and second row will share the available space within the container.)

`repeat()` Notation:

- A shorthand for repeating track definitions. `repeat(3, 1fr)` is the same as `1fr 1fr 1fr`.
- You can use `auto-fill` or `auto-fit` with `repeat()` and `minmax()` to create responsive, automatic grids without explicit media queries initially.
  - `auto-fill`: Creates as many columns/rows as can fit without overflowing, even if there aren't enough items to fill them all (empty tracks are created).
  - `auto-fit`: Similar to `auto-fill`, but it collapses empty tracks. This is often more desirable.
- Example: `grid-template-columns: repeat(auto-fit, minmax(200px, 1fr));` This creates as many columns as possible, each at least 200px wide but growing to fill the space equally (`1fr`) if space is available.

Example with `repeat` and `auto-fit`:

```css
.responsive-grid {
  display: grid;
  /* Create responsive columns: as many as fit, each at least 200px,
max 1fr */
  grid-template-columns: repeat(auto-fit, minmax(200px, 1fr));
  gap: 15px; /* Gap between items */
  padding: 15px;
  border: 2px solid orange;
}


.responsive-grid > div {
  background-color: lightyellow;
  border: 1px solid darkorange;
  padding: 20px;
  text-align: center;
}
```

(Result: The items will automatically arrange themselves into rows and columns. On a wide screen, you might see 4 or 5 columns. As you narrow the browser, the columns will shrink until they hit 200px, at which point an item will "wrap" to the next row, reducing the number of columns to 3, then 2, then maybe 1 on a very narrow screen. No media queries needed for this basic responsiveness!)

`column-gap`, `row-gap`, and `gap` (Shorthand)

- Adds space (gutters) *between* the grid tracks (rows and columns). They **do not** add space outside the grid.
- `column-gap`: Space between columns.
- `row-gap`: Space between rows.
- `gap`: Shorthand for `row-gap column-gap`. If only one value is provided, it applies to both.

Personal Insight: The `fr` unit and `repeat(auto-fit, minmax(value, 1fr))` are incredibly powerful for building flexible, responsive grid layouts without manual breakpoints for every column change. I use this pattern constantly for things like card grids or lists of products.

4.3 Placing Grid Items Explicitly (`grid-row`, `grid-column`)

By default, grid items are automatically placed row by row, filling the grid. But often, you need specific items to go into specific cells or span multiple cells. You do this by referencing the **grid lines**.

Grid lines are numbered implicitly starting from 1.

- Vertical lines: 1, 2, 3, ... (from left to right)
- Horizontal lines: 1, 2, 3, ... (from top to bottom)

You can place an item using the `grid-row-start`, `grid-row-end`, `grid-column-start`, and `grid-column-end` properties on the **Grid Item**.

```css
.grid-container-placement {
  display: grid;
  grid-template-columns: 100px 100px 100px; /* Lines 1, 2, 3, 4
vertically */
  grid-template-rows: 50px 50px 50px;       /* Lines 1, 2, 3, 4
horizontally */
  gap: 10px;
  border: 2px solid blue;
}


.item-a {
  background-color: lightblue;
  /* Place this item starting at vertical line 1, ending at vertical
line 3 */
  grid-column-start: 1;
  grid-column-end: 3; /* Spans across 2 columns (from line 1 to line
3) */
```

```
  /* Place this item starting at horizontal line 2, ending at
horizontal line 4 */
  grid-row-start: 2;
  grid-row-end: 4; /* Spans across 2 rows (from line 2 to line 4) */
}


.item-b {
  background-color: lightgreen;
  /* Place this item in the top-right cell (from column line 3 to 4,
row line 1 to 2) */
  grid-column-start: 3;
  grid-column-end: 4; /* Could also use `grid-column-end: span 1;` */
  grid-row-start: 1;
  grid-row-end: 2; /* Could also use `grid-row-end: span 1;` */
}


/* Other items would auto-place around these explicitly placed ones */

<!-- HTML -->
<div class="grid-container-placement">
  <div class="grid-item item-a">Item A (Spans)</div>
  <div class="grid-item item-b">Item B</div>
  <div class="grid-item">Item 3</div>
  <div class="grid-item">Item 4</div>
  <div class="grid-item">Item 5</div>
  <div class="grid-item">Item 6</div>
</div>
```

(Result: Item A will stretch from the top-left corner of the second row down to the bottom-right corner of the third row, spanning two columns and two rows. Item B will sit in the top-right cell. The other items will try to auto-place in the remaining empty cells.)

Shorthands: `grid-column`, `grid-row`, and `grid-area`

- `grid-column: start-line / end-line;` (e.g., `grid-column: 1 / 3;`)
- `grid-row: start-line / end-line;` (e.g., `grid-row: 2 / 4;`)
- You can also use `span count` instead of the end line number (e.g., `grid-column: 1 / span 2;` is equivalent to `grid-column: 1 / 3;`).

- grid-area: start-row / start-column / end-row / end-column; (e.g., grid-area: 2 / 1 / 4 / 3; - same as Item A above). This is a very useful shorthand!

4.4 Aligning Items Within the Grid (justify-items, align-items, place-items, justify-content, align-content, place-content)

Grid has its own set of alignment properties, similar in name to Flexbox but applied slightly differently because you're working within a 2D grid of cells.

Alignment *within* Cells (Applied to the Grid Container):

These properties align the **content** of the grid items *inside their grid cells*.

- **justify-items**: Aligns items along the **inline axis** (usually horizontal) within their cells.
  - Values: start, end, center, stretch (default)
- **align-items**: Aligns items along the **block axis** (usually vertical) within their cells.
  - Values: start, end, center, stretch (default), baseline
- **place-items**: Shorthand for align-items justify-items. If only one value, it applies to both. (e.g., place-items: center;)

Example:

```
.container-cell-align {
  display: grid;
  grid-template-columns: repeat(3, 100px);
  grid-template-rows: repeat(2, 80px);
  gap: 10px;
  border: 2px solid green;

  /* Align all items within their cells */
  justify-items: center; /* Center horizontally in cell */
  align-items: center;   /* Center vertically in cell */
  /* Or use shorthand: place-items: center; */
}


.container-cell-align > div {
  background-color: lightgreen;
  border: 1px solid darkgreen;
  padding: 5px;
}
```

(Result: Each item will be centered both horizontally and vertically within its 100x80px grid cell.)

Alignment of the *Grid Itself* (Applied to the Grid Container):

These properties align the **entire grid block** within the grid container if the grid is *smaller* than the container. They distribute extra space around the grid.

- **justify-content**: Aligns the grid along the **inline axis** (usually horizontal).
  - Values: start, end, center, space-between, space-around, space-evenly, stretch (default)
- **align-content**: Aligns the grid along the **block axis** (usually vertical).
  - Values: start, end, center, space-between, space-around, space-evenly, stretch (default)
- **place-content**: Shorthand for align-content justify-content. If only one value, applies to both. (e.g., place-content: center;)

Example (assuming container is larger than the grid):

```
.container-grid-align {
  display: grid;
  grid-template-columns: repeat(3, 80px); /* Total grid width = 240px
+ gaps */
  grid-template-rows: repeat(2, 60px);    /* Total grid height = 120px
+ gaps */
  gap: 10px;
  border: 2px solid orange;
  width: 400px; /* Container wider than grid */
  height: 300px; /* Container taller than grid */

  /* Align the entire grid within the container */
  justify-content: center; /* Center grid horizontally */
  align-content: center;   /* Center grid vertically */
  /* Or shorthand: place-content: center; */
}


.container-grid-align > div {
  background-color: lightyellow;
  border: 1px solid darkorange;
  padding: 5px;
}
```

C

(Result: The entire 3x2 grid block (including items and gaps) will be centered both horizontally and vertically within the larger orange container.)

Alignment of a *Single Item* within its Cell (Applied to the Grid Item):

These properties override the `justify-items` and `align-items` set on the container for a specific item.

- **`justify-self`**: Aligns a single item along the **inline axis** (horizontal) within *its own* cell.
  - Values: `start`, `end`, `center`, `stretch` (default), `auto`
- **`align-self`**: Aligns a single item along the **block axis** (vertical) within *its own* cell.
  - Values: `start`, `end`, `center`, `stretch` (default), `auto`, `baseline`
- **`place-self`**: Shorthand for `align-self justify-self`.

Example:

```css
.container-self-align {
  display: grid;
  grid-template-columns: repeat(3, 100px);
  grid-template-rows: repeat(2, 80px);
  gap: 10px;
  border: 2px solid purple;
  /* Optional: Set container alignment, then override on an item */
  /* place-items: start; */
}


.container-self-align > div {
  background-color: #eee;
  border: 1px solid #ccc;
  padding: 5px;
  /* Optional: Default alignment from container */
  /* align-items: start; justify-items: start; */
}


.item-special {
  background-color: lightblue;
  justify-self: end; /* Align this item to the right within its cell */
  align-self: center;   /* Align this item to the vertical center within its cell */
```

```
}
<!-- HTML -->
<div class="container-self-align">
  <div>Item 1</div>
  <div class="item-special">Special Item</div>
  <div>Item 3</div>
  <div>Item 4</div>
</div>
```

(Result: Item 2 will be aligned to the bottom-right of its cell (assuming default container alignment is stretch or start) or horizontally to the end and vertically centered, regardless of how the other items are aligned by the container's `place-items`.)

Personal Insight: The Grid alignment properties can be confusing because of the sheer number and the similar names to Flexbox. My mental model is: the properties ending in `-items` or `-self` control alignment *inside* the grid cells. The properties ending in `-content` control alignment of the *entire grid* block within its container when there's extra space. And remember `place-items` and `place-content` for the useful shorthands!

4.5 Naming Grid Areas for Readability

While placing items by line numbers is powerful, it can become hard to read and maintain for complex layouts. CSS Grid offers a more visual and semantic way using **Grid Areas**.

1. Define your grid structure *and* name the areas within it using the `grid-template-areas` property on the **Grid Container**. You visually "draw" your layout using strings.

   Each string represents a row, and the names within the string represent the area names, separated by spaces. A period (.) signifies an empty cell.

2. Place a grid item into a named area using the `grid-area` property on the **Grid Item**, giving it the name you defined in step 1.

Example: A Classic "Holy Grail" Layout (Header, Sidebar, Main, Footer)

```
<!-- HTML -->
<div class="holy-grail-layout">
  <header class="header">Header</header>
  <aside class="sidebar">Sidebar</aside>
  <main class="main">Main Content</main>
  <footer class="footer">Footer</footer>
</div>

/* CSS */
```

```css
.holy-grail-layout {
  display: grid;
  min-height: 100vh; /* Make container at least viewport height */
  gap: 10px; /* Space between areas */
  padding: 10px; /* Padding around the whole layout */
  border: 2px solid blue;

  /* Define the grid structure and name the areas VISUALLY */
  grid-template-columns: 200px 1fr; /* 2 columns: 200px wide sidebar,
rest (1fr) for main */
  grid-template-rows: auto 1fr auto; /* 3 rows: auto-height header,
1fr for main/sidebar area, auto-height footer */
  grid-template-areas:
    "header  header"  /* Row 1: header spans both columns */
    "sidebar main"    /* Row 2: sidebar in col 1, main in col 2 */
    "footer  footer"; /* Row 3: footer spans both columns */
}

/* Assign items to the named areas */
.header { grid-area: header; background-color: lightblue; }
.sidebar { grid-area: sidebar; background-color: lightgreen; }
.main { grid-area: main; background-color: lightcoral; }
.footer { grid-area: footer; background-color: lightyellow; }

/* Add some padding to items for visibility */
.holy-grail-layout > * {
  padding: 15px;
  border: 1px solid black;
}
```

(Result: A full-page layout with a header spanning the top, a footer spanning the bottom, and a sidebar next to the main content area in between. Changing the `grid-template-areas` *string literally redraws the layout!)*

Personal Insight: `grid-template-areas` is incredibly intuitive once you get the hang of it. It's like drawing your layout in CSS code. For major page regions or complex, static component layouts, it often leads to much more readable and maintainable CSS than using line numbers, especially when combined with media queries to redefine the areas for different screen sizes.

4.6 Practical Grid Layouts for Sections, Dashboards, and more

Grid is your tool for building:

- **Full Page Layouts:** Header, footer, navigation, sidebar, main content (like the Holy Grail example).
- **Section Layouts:** A section with text on the left and an image on the right, a multi-column feature list, a blog post layout with an author bio sidebar.
- **Dashboards:** Arranging various widgets or data panels in a structured grid.
- **Any 2D Structure:** Anything that conceptually fits into rows and columns.

Responsive Grid with Areas:

One of the most powerful aspects is changing the grid structure (columns, rows, *and* areas) with media queries.

```css
/* Using the holy-grail-layout example */

/* Default layout (e.g., mobile-first, single column) */
.holy-grail-layout {
  display: grid;
  min-height: 100vh;
  gap: 10px;
  padding: 10px;
  grid-template-columns: 1fr; /* Single column */
  grid-template-rows: auto auto 1fr auto; /* Header, sidebar, main
(takes space), footer */
  grid-template-areas:
    "header"
    "sidebar" /* Sidebar above main on mobile */
    "main"
    "footer";
}

/* Desktop layout */
@media (min-width: 768px) { /* When screen is at least 768px wide */
  .holy-grail-layout {
    grid-template-columns: 200px 1fr; /* Two columns */
    grid-template-rows: auto 1fr auto; /* Header, main/sidebar area,
footer */
    grid-template-areas:
      "header  header"
```

```
    "sidebar main"   /* Sidebar next to main on desktop */
    "footer  footer";
  }
}


/* Item assignment stays the same! */
.header { grid-area: header; background-color: lightblue; }
.sidebar { grid-area: sidebar; background-color: lightgreen; }
.main { grid-area: main; background-color: lightcoral; }
.footer { grid-area: footer; background-color: lightyellow; }
```

(Result: On smaller screens, the elements stack vertically based on the first `grid-template-areas` definition. On screens 768px and wider, the grid structure and areas completely change to the two-column layout, simply by redefining the container properties in the media query. This makes building complex responsive layouts incredibly efficient!)

Grid and Flexbox are not mutually exclusive. You'll often use Flexbox *inside* a Grid item to align content within that cell (e.g., using Flexbox to center text inside a grid cell, or creating a button group within a dashboard panel placed by Grid). They are powerful complements.

Chapter 4 Summary

You've taken a significant step in modern CSS layout by exploring CSS Grid:

- You understand the key terminology: **Grid Container**, **Grid Items**, **Grid Lines**, **Grid Tracks** (Rows/Columns), **Grid Cells**, and **Grid Areas**.
- You know how to define the grid structure using `display: grid;` and `grid-template-columns` / `grid-template-rows`, including the powerful `fr` unit, `repeat()`, and `minmax()`.
- You learned how to add space between tracks using `gap` (or `column-gap`, `row-gap`).
- You explored how to explicitly place grid items using line numbers with `grid-column` and `grid-row` (and the `grid-area` shorthand for line-based placement).
- You delved into Grid's alignment properties (`justify-items`, `align-items`, `place-items` for items in cells; `justify-content`, `align-content`, `place-content` for the grid block; `justify-self`, `align-self`, `place-self` for individual items).
- You learned how to define and use **Named Grid Areas** with `grid-template-areas` and `grid-area` for highly readable layouts.
- You saw examples of practical Grid layouts and how Grid works seamlessly with media queries for responsiveness.

Grid is complex, but incredibly rewarding. It gives you precise control over your 2D layouts. Like Flexbox, the best way to learn is by doing. Create grid containers, define columns and rows, place items, and play with the alignment properties. Use your browser's developer tools – they have fantastic visual overlays that show you the grid lines, track sizes, and areas, which is invaluable for debugging and understanding.

Chapter 5: Responsive Web Design: Adapting to Any Device

Think about how you browse the web today. Are you always on a desktop computer? Probably not! You might be on your phone during your commute, on a tablet on the couch, maybe even a smart TV or a gaming console's browser. Devices come in all shapes and sizes, with vastly different screen dimensions and interaction methods (mouse vs. touch).

If your website looks fantastic on your big monitor but requires painful zooming and side-scrolling on a phone, users are going to bail. Fast. This is where **Responsive Web Design (RWD)** comes in.

RWD isn't a single technology; it's an approach, a philosophy, backed by specific CSS techniques that allow your website's layout and design to automatically adapt to the user's screen size, resolution, and orientation. The goal? To provide an optimal viewing and interaction experience for everyone, everywhere.

5.1 The Philosophy of Responsive Design and Mobile-First

Before we write any code, let's talk about the mindset. Historically, developers built websites for desktop screens first, then tried to shrink them down for smaller devices. This often led to complex, hacky code to hide or rearrange elements.

The modern, and often more effective, approach is **Mobile-First**.

What is Mobile-First?

It means you start designing and coding for the *smallest* screen size (typically a smartphone) first. You build the core content and layout that works well on a narrow screen. Only *then* do you progressively enhance the design for larger screens using CSS.

Why Mobile-First is Often Preferred:

1. **Performance:** Mobile devices often have slower connections and less processing power. By starting mobile-first, you're forced to prioritize content and performance from the get-go. You load only what's necessary for a mobile view and add more complex styles and layouts *conditionally* for larger screens.
2. **Content Focus:** Mobile screens have limited real estate. Designing for mobile first encourages you to focus on the most important content and primary calls to action. You strip away clutter early in the process.
3. **Simpler CSS:** With mobile-first, your base CSS styles are for the small screen. You then use media queries (which we'll get to shortly) to *add* or *override* styles *only* when the screen is large enough. This often results in cleaner, more maintainable CSS compared to starting with desktop styles and trying to *undo* them for mobile.
4. **Progressive Enhancement:** You start with a solid, usable experience on the most constrained devices and add richer experiences as screen capabilities increase.

Personal Insight: I resisted mobile-first initially. It felt backwards! But after a few projects where shrinking a complex desktop layout for mobile was a constant battle, I switched. Building up from mobile feels much more natural now. You define the default, stacked, simple layout first, and then use media queries almost like checkboxes: "IF the screen is wide enough, THEN arrange these items horizontally," "IF the screen is wide enough, THEN show this sidebar." It genuinely simplifies the CSS logic.

This doesn't mean you ignore desktop designs entirely. You still need to know what the final layout looks like. But the *coding process* starts with the constraints of the smallest screen.

5.2 Setting the Viewport Meta Tag

Okay, philosophy in place, let's talk about a non-negotiable piece of HTML you need for RWD to even work correctly: the viewport meta tag.

Have you ever visited a website on your phone and noticed it looked like a tiny version of the desktop site, where you had to pinch-to-zoom just to read anything? That happens when the browser thinks its viewport (the area where the webpage is displayed) is much larger than the actual device screen. It renders the site at a wide desktop width, then just shrinks the result to fit the small screen. Not a great experience!

The `<meta name="viewport">` tag, placed in the `<head>` of your HTML document, tells the browser how to control the page's dimensions and scaling. For responsive design, you almost always want this:

```
<!-- Add this inside the <head> section of your HTML -->
<meta name="viewport" content="width=device-width, initial-scale=1.0">
```

Let's break down the `content` attribute values:

- `width=device-width`: This sets the width of the viewport to the width of the device's screen in CSS pixels. This is key! It tells the browser, "Hey, the `100%` width I use in my CSS should refer to the *actual* width of this screen, not some large default."
- `initial-scale=1.0`: This sets the initial zoom level when the page is first loaded. `1.0` means no zoom is applied. This ensures that 1 CSS pixel roughly equals 1 device pixel initially, preventing that zoomed-out look.

Without this meta tag, your media queries might not work as expected, and elements sized with percentages or viewport units might not scale correctly. So, make it a habit: whenever you start a new HTML file, put that viewport meta tag in the `<head>`.

5.3 Implementing Responsive Behavior with Media Queries

The workhorse of Responsive Web Design in CSS is the **Media Query**. A media query allows you to apply CSS styles selectively, only when certain conditions (or "media features") are met. The most common condition is the width of the viewport.

The basic syntax looks like this:

```css
/* Styles outside the media query apply always (or to the base/mobile
view) */
body {
  background-color: lightblue; /* Default background */
}


/* Media query: Apply styles only if the screen is at least 768px wide
*/
@media screen and (min-width: 768px) {
  /* Styles inside here only apply on screens 768px or wider */
  body {
    background-color: lightgreen; /* Change background on wider
screens */
  }

  /* You can change any CSS property here */
  .my-element {
    width: 50%; /* Make this element half width on wider screens */
    float: left; /* Maybe make it float for a side-by-side layout */
  }
}


/* Another media query: Apply styles only if the screen is between
768px and 1024px wide */
@media screen and (min-width: 768px) and (max-width: 1024px) {
  .some-other-element {
    font-size: 1.1rem; /* Slightly larger font size on medium screens
*/
  }
}
```

Let's break down the components:

- `@media`: The rule that starts the media query.

- `screen`: Specifies the media type (you can also have `print` for print styles, `speech`, etc. `screen` is most common for RWD).
- `and`: Combines multiple conditions.
- `(min-width: 768px)`: This is the "media feature" or condition. It means "only apply these styles if the viewport width is **at least** 768 pixels." This is typical for a mobile-first approach – styles *outside* the query are for <768px, styles *inside* are for >=768px.
- `(max-width: 1023px)`: This means "only apply these styles if the viewport width is **at most** 1023 pixels."
- `{ ... }`: The declaration block containing the CSS rules that will be applied when the condition(s) are true.

Common Media Features for RWD:
- `width` / `min-width` / `max-width`: Most common for adapting layout to screen size.
- `height` / `min-height` / `max-height`: Less common for overall layout, but useful if a design needs to change based on viewport height.
- `orientation`: `portrait` or `landscape`. Useful for changing layouts based on how a tablet or phone is held. `@media screen and (orientation: landscape) { ... }`

Setting Breakpoints:
The pixel values you use in `min-width` or `max-width` are called **breakpoints**. These are the points where your design "breaks" or changes significantly.

- **Device-driven breakpoints:** Historically, people might have used breakpoints based on common device sizes (e.g., 320px for old iPhones, 768px for tablets, 1024px for desktops). This is less ideal now due to the sheer number of devices.
- **Content-driven breakpoints:** A better approach is to let your *content* dictate where breakpoints are needed. Start with your mobile layout. As you widen your browser window, look for the point where the layout starts to look awkward, lines of text get too long, or elements bump into each other. *That's* where you need a breakpoint to adjust the layout (e.g., introduce columns, increase padding, show a sidebar). This results in a design that adapts well regardless of whether the user has a specific "standard" device size.

Example: Changing a Simple Stacked Layout to a Two-Column Layout

```html
<!-- HTML -->
<div class="responsive-container">
  <div class="box">Box 1</div>
  <div class="box">Box 2</div>
</div>
```

```css
/* CSS (Mobile-First - default is stacked) */
.responsive-container {
  border: 2px solid blue;
  padding: 10px;
}

.box {
  background-color: lightblue;
  border: 1px solid navy;
  padding: 10px;
  margin-bottom: 10px; /* Space when stacked */
}

/* Desktop breakpoint: Switch to a two-column layout using Flexbox */
@media (min-width: 600px) {
  .responsive-container {
    display: flex; /* Turn container into flex container */
    gap: 10px;     /* Add space between boxes */
  }

  .box {
    flex: 1; /* Make boxes take up equal space */
    margin-bottom: 0; /* Remove bottom margin when in a row */
  }
}
```

(Result: Below 600px, the boxes stack vertically with margin at the bottom. At 600px and wider, the container becomes a flex container, and the boxes sit side-by-side, each taking up half the width, with a gap between them.)

This simple example shows how you define the base style (stacked, margin-bottom) *first*, and then use a media query to *override* those styles (`display: flex;`, `gap:`, `margin-bottom: 0;`) only when the screen is wide enough. This is the essence of mobile-first and media queries working together.

5.4 Creating Flexible Images and Media

Images and videos can easily break responsive layouts if they're wider than their container. The simplest, most common fix is to make them flexible.

```css
/* Make images and videos scale down proportionally if they are too big */
```

```
img, video {
  max-width: 100%; /* Ensure element is never wider than its container
*/
  height: auto;    /* Maintain aspect ratio by adjusting height
automatically */
}
```

Applying this simple rule means that if an image's original width is, say, 800px, but its container is only 500px wide, the image will shrink down to 500px (because `max-width: 100%` limits it to the container's width). The `height: auto;` ensures it shrinks proportionally, preventing distortion. If the container is wider than the original image (e.g., 1000px container, 800px image), the image will only take up its original 800px, as `max-width` doesn't force it to grow beyond 100% of *itself* (unless its container is smaller).

More Advanced Responsive Images:

For truly optimized responsive images (serving different image files or sizes based on resolution or viewport), you'd use HTML features like the `<picture>` element and the `srcset` attribute on `<img>` tags. While this is more HTML than CSS, it's a crucial part of the responsive image puzzle for performance. CSS handles the *layout* of the image, but HTML can handle *which* image file is loaded.

5.5 Techniques for Responsive Typography

Text needs to be readable on tiny phone screens and large desktop monitors. This means controlling `font-size`, `line-height`, and potentially `line-width`.

- **Relative Units:** Instead of using fixed `px` units for font sizes (which don't scale well if users change browser font settings), use relative units:
    - em: Relative to the font size of the *parent* element.
    - rem: Relative to the font size of the *root* (`<html>`) element. (Generally preferred as it's easier to manage).
    - vw: Relative to the viewport width (1vw is 1% of the viewport width).

```
/* Set a base font size on the root (html) */
html {
  font-size: 100%; /* 100% of default browser font size (usually 16px)
*/
  /* You could change this in a media query */
  /* @media (min-width: 800px) { font-size: 112.5%; /* Base becomes
18px */ } */
}
```

```css
body {
  font-size: 1rem; /* This will be 16px (from html) */
  line-height: 1.5; /* 1.5 times the font-size */
}


h1 {
  font-size: 2.5rem; /* 2.5 times the base (40px) */
  /* Could make this fluid: */
  /* font-size: calc(1.5rem + 2vw); /* Mix of rem and vw for fluid
scaling */
}


@media (min-width: 1000px) {
  body {
    line-height: 1.6; /* Increase line height on wider screens for
readability */
  }
}
```

- **Fluid Typography with `clamp()`:** A modern CSS function (`clamp(min, preferred, max)`) lets you set a font size that scales fluidly between a minimum and maximum size based on the viewport width.
  - `font-size: clamp(1rem, 2vw + 0.5rem, 2rem);` means the font size will be *at least* 1rem, *at most* 2rem, and will scale based on `2vw + 0.5rem` in between.
- **Line Length:** On very wide screens, lines of text can become too long to read comfortably. You might use `max-width` on your text containers to keep line lengths manageable (around 50-75 characters per line is often cited as ideal).

5.6 Combining Flexbox and Grid for Responsive Components

This is where the power of the modern layout modules truly shines in RWD. Flexbox and Grid are inherently designed to be flexible.

- **Flexbox (`flex-wrap` & `flex`):** We saw this in Chapter 3. Setting `display: flex;` on a container and `flex-wrap: wrap;` combined with flexible `flex-basis` values or the `flex: 1;` shorthand on items makes items automatically adjust their size and flow to the next line as space changes, without needing explicit breakpoints for every minor adjustment. You only need breakpoints for major layout shifts (e.g., when a row of items becomes a column stack).
- **Grid (`fr`, `repeat(auto-fit, minmax())`, `grid-template-areas`):** As shown in Chapter 4, the `fr` unit allows columns/rows to share available space proportionally. `repeat(auto-fit, minmax(..., 1fr))` creates highly flexible,

automatic responsive grids. And perhaps most powerfully, you can completely redefine your `grid-template-columns`, `grid-template-rows`, and even `grid-template-areas` within media queries to achieve dramatic layout changes at different breakpoints, keeping your HTML structure clean.

Personal Insight: Learning to leverage `flex-wrap: wrap;` and `repeat(auto-fit, minmax(..., 1fr));` significantly reduced the number of breakpoints I needed in my CSS. Instead of writing queries for every possible screen width, I now use them primarily for the main structural shifts (e.g., single column mobile -> sidebar + main desktop) and let Flexbox and Grid handle the fluid adjustments in between.

By combining these tools, you can build components and entire page layouts that not only look good on one screen size but intelligently adapt across the vast spectrum of devices your users might be on.

Chapter 5 Summary

Responsive Web Design is essential for building modern websites. You've learned:

- The importance of **Responsive Web Design** and the benefits of adopting a **Mobile-First** development approach.
- The critical role of the **Viewport Meta Tag** (`<meta name="viewport" content="width=device-width, initial-scale=1.0">`) in controlling scaling.
- How **Media Queries** (`@media`) allow you to apply styles conditionally based on characteristics like screen width (`min-width`, `max-width`).
- Techniques for making **Images and Media Flexible** using `max-width: 100%; height: auto;`.
- Strategies for **Responsive Typography** using relative units (`rem`, `vw`) and functions like `clamp()`.
- How **Flexbox and Grid Layouts** are inherently responsive tools that significantly simplify building adaptive designs.

You now have the fundamental tools to start making your layouts respond to different screen sizes. Practice creating simple layouts and applying media queries to change their appearance at different widths. Use your browser's developer tools to resize the window and see your designs adapt!

Chapter 6: Styling Text, Color, and Backgrounds

You've got your elements structured with HTML, and you're learning how to arrange them on the page using Flexbox and Grid. That's a huge leap! But a page with perfect layout but plain black text on a white background isn't going to grab anyone's attention or guide them effectively.

This chapter is all about controlling the visual presentation of your content itself and the elements it lives within. We'll explore everything from choosing the right font to applying vibrant colors and dynamic backgrounds. Getting this right is crucial not just for aesthetics, but for usability, readability, and reinforcing your brand or message.

6.1 Working with Typography: Font Properties, Units, and Web Fonts

Typography is arguably one of the most important aspects of web design. Most web content is text! Choosing the right fonts and styling them appropriately can make the difference between a frustrating reading experience and an enjoyable one.

Let's start with the fundamental font properties:

`font-family`

- This specifies the typeface you want to use. Browsers can only display fonts that are available on the user's computer or explicitly provided as web fonts.
- You list multiple font names as a "font stack," separated by commas. The browser will try to load the first font in the list, then the second, and so on, until it finds one it can use.
- Always end your font stack with a **generic font family** (`serif`, `sans-serif`, `monospace`, `cursive`, `fantasy`). This ensures *some* font from that category is used as a final fallback if none of the specific fonts are available.

```css
/* Use Lato if available, otherwise Arial, otherwise any sans-serif
font */
body {
  font-family: 'Lato', Arial, sans-serif;
}


/* Use Georgia if available, otherwise Times New Roman, otherwise any
serif font */
h1 {
  font-family: Georgia, 'Times New Roman', serif;
}


/* Use a monospace font for code snippets */
pre, code {
  font-family: 'Courier New', Courier, monospace;
```

```
}
```

font-size

- Sets the size of the text. Getting this right is crucial for readability on different devices.
- Avoid using `px` for all font sizes, especially on body text. Relative units are preferred for responsiveness and accessibility.
  - **px**: Fixed pixel size. Predictable, but doesn't scale if the user changes their browser's base font size settings. Good for elements where exact pixel size is critical (rare).
  - **em**: Relative to the `font-size` of the *parent* element. Can be tricky as it compounds – an `em` size on a child inside a parent with an `em` size can be hard to predict.
  - **rem**: Relative to the `font-size` of the *root* (`<html>`) element. This is generally the most recommended unit for font sizes because it provides consistent scaling relative to one base value. If you set `html { font-size: 100%; }` (which is usually the default 16px), then `1rem` is 16px, `1.5rem` is 24px, etc. If you change the root font size in a media query (e.g., `html { font-size: 112.5%; /* 18px */ }` for larger screens), all `rem` units scale accordingly.
  - **vw**: Relative to the viewport width (1vw is 1% of the viewport width). Can be used for "fluid typography" where text size scales smoothly as the browser window resizes. Often used in combination with other units (see `clamp()` in Chapter 5).

```
/* Set base font size on the root */
html {
  font-size: 100%; /* Default browser size, usually 16px */
}


body {
  font-size: 1rem; /* 16px */
}


h1 {
  font-size: 2.5rem; /* 40px */
}


.small-text {
  font-size: 0.875rem; /* 14px */
}
```

```
/* Example of using em (can compound) */
.parent { font-size: 20px; }
.parent .child { font-size: 0.8em; /* 80% of 20px = 16px */ }
```

font-weight

- Sets the thickness (or boldness) of the text.
- Values: `normal` (usually 400), `bold` (usually 700), and numerical values from `100` to `900` (in multiples of 100). Not all fonts support all weight values.

```
p {
    font-weight: normal;
}


strong {
    font-weight: bold;
}


.light-text {
    font-weight: 300; /* If the font supports it */
}
```

font-style

- Sets whether the text is italic.
- Values: `normal, italic, oblique`. `italic` is more common and usually preferred.

font-variant

- Allows rendering text in small caps.
- Value: `small-caps`.

font (Shorthand)

- A shorthand property to set multiple font properties in a single declaration.
- Order matters: `font-style font-variant font-weight font-size/line-height font-family`. `font-size` and `font-family` are required.

```
/* Normal 400 weight, 16px size, with a line height 1.5 times the font
size, using Arial */
p {
    font: normal 400 1rem/1.5 Arial, sans-serif;
```

```
}
```

Personal Insight: Using the `font` shorthand can be efficient, but I sometimes prefer listing properties individually (`font-size`, `line-family`, etc.) for clarity, especially in larger style sheets. It makes it easier to see and adjust just one property without having to parse the whole shorthand. It's a matter of team preference, but consistency is key!

Web Fonts (`@font-face`)

Using fonts that aren't typically installed on a user's computer (like custom brand fonts or popular Google Fonts) requires embedding them. The most common way is via `@font-face`.

You define the font family name you want to use in your CSS and tell the browser where to find the font files.

```css
/* Define a custom font */
@font-face {
  font-family: 'MyCustomFont'; /* Name you'll use in font-family */
  src: url('mycustomfont.woff2') format('woff2'), /* Path to font
files */
       url('mycustomfont.woff') format('woff');
  font-weight: normal;
  font-style: normal;
}


/* Use the custom font */
h1 {
  font-family: 'MyCustomFont', sans-serif;
}
```

content_copydownload

Use code with caution.Css

Browsers support different font file formats (`.woff`, `.woff2`, `.ttf`, `.otf`, `.eot`, `.svg`). `.woff2` is the most modern and generally has the best compression. Providing multiple formats in the `src` list ensures broader browser compatibility.

Using Google Fonts:

Google Fonts is a popular, easy way to include web fonts hosted by Google. You typically add a `<link>` tag to your HTML `<head>` provided by Google, and then you can use the font family name in your CSS.

```html
<!-- Add this to your <head> -->
<link rel="preconnect" href="https://fonts.googleapis.com">
<link rel="preconnect" href="https://fonts.gstatic.com" crossorigin>
<link href="https://fonts.googleapis.com/css2?family=Roboto:wght@400;700&display=swap" rel="stylesheet">

/* Then use the font in your CSS */
body {
  font-family: 'Roboto', sans-serif;
}
```

This is simpler than managing `@font-face` yourself, but relies on a third-party service.

Personal Insight: Web fonts are fantastic for design, but be mindful of performance. Each font file needs to be downloaded by the user's browser. Using too many different fonts, weights, or styles can slow down page loading. Consider sticking to 1-2 font families and only including the weights you actually need (e.g., 400 and 700). The `display=swap` parameter in the Google Fonts link is important for performance – it tells the browser to use a fallback font first and swap in the web font when it's loaded, preventing invisible text during loading.

6.2 Styling Text Content: Alignment, Decoration, Spacing, and Transformation

Beyond the font itself, you can control how the text within an element is rendered.

`text-align`

- Controls the horizontal alignment of inline content (like text and inline/inline-block elements) within a block-level container.
- Values: `left`, `right`, `center`, `justify`.

```css
.intro-paragraph {
  text-align: center; /* Center the text within this element */
}


.blog-article {
```

```
    text-align: justify; /* Spread text to fill the line, creating crisp
edges */
}
```

Personal Insight: Be cautious with `text-align: justify` on web content, especially in narrow columns. It can sometimes create awkward gaps between words ("rivers") which reduce readability. Left alignment is often safer and easier to read for main body text.

text-decoration

- Adds lines to text. Most commonly used to remove the default underline from links.
- Values: `none, underline, overline, line-through`. You can also control color and style (`text-decoration: underline dashed red;`).

```
a {
    text-decoration: none; /* Remove underline from links */
}
```

```
.strike {
    text-decoration: line-through; /* Cross out text */
}
```

text-transform

- Changes the casing of text without altering the HTML.
- Values: `none` (default), `uppercase` (ALL CAPS), `lowercase` (all lowercase), `capitalize` (Capitalize Each Word).

```
h1 {
    text-transform: uppercase;
}
```

```
.caption {
    text-transform: lowercase;
}
```

letter-spacing and word-spacing

- Adjusts the spacing between characters (`letter-spacing`) or words (`word-spacing`). Can be positive or negative values. Use sparingly, as overly tight or loose spacing hurts readability.

```
h1 {
  letter-spacing: 2px; /* Add space between letters */
}


.title {
  word-spacing: 0.5em; /* Add space between words */
}
```

line-height

- Sets the height of each line of text. This is CRUCIAL for readability! Too little space makes text feel cramped; too much makes it hard for the eye to track from the end of one line to the start of the next.
- Best practice is usually to use a **unitless number** (e.g., `1.5`). This number is multiplied by the element's *own* `font-size` to determine the line height. This ensures consistent relative spacing even if nested elements have different font sizes (as opposed to using `px` or `em` which can lead to compounding or inconsistent gaps). A value between `1.4` and `1.6` is often a good starting point for body text.

```
p {
  line-height: 1.5; /* Line height is 1.5 times the paragraph's font-size */
}
```

text-shadow

- Adds a shadow effect to text. Values are `offset-x offset-y blur-radius color`.

```
h1 {
  text-shadow: 2px 2px 4px rgba(0, 0, 0, 0.5); /* Horizontal offset, Vertical offset, Blur, Color (with transparency) */
}
```

white-space

- Controls how whitespace within an element is handled.

- Values include `normal` (collapse multiple spaces, wrap lines), `nowrap` (don't wrap lines), `pre` (like `<pre>` tag, preserves whitespace and line breaks), `pre-wrap` (preserves whitespace, wraps lines), `pre-line` (collapses whitespace, preserves line breaks).

`text-overflow`

- Controls how overflowing text is signaled to the user. Requires `white-space: nowrap;` and `overflow: hidden;` on the element.
- Value: `ellipsis` is common (`...`).

```css
.single-line-ellipsis {
  white-space: nowrap; /* Prevent wrapping */
  overflow: hidden;    /* Hide overflow */
  text-overflow: ellipsis; /* Show ellipsis for hidden text */
  width: 200px; /* Needs a fixed width or max-width to demonstrate */
}
```

6.3 Understanding Color Models (Hex, RGB, HSL)

Adding color is one of the most direct ways to impact a design's look and feel. CSS allows you to specify colors in several ways.

- **Named Colors:** Simple, predefined color names (e.g., `red`, `blue`, `white`, `black`, `tomato`, `steelblue`). Limited palette.
- **Hexadecimal (Hex):** A 6-digit (or 3-digit shorthand) code representing Red, Green, and Blue values, prefixed with `#`. Each pair/digit ranges from `00` to `FF` (0 to 255 in decimal).
  - `#RRGGBB`: Full form (e.g., `#FF0000` is red, `#00FF00` is green, `#0000FF` is blue, `#000000` is black, `#FFFFFF` is white).
  - `#RGB`: Shorthand (e.g., `#F00` is `#FF0000`, `#0F0` is `#00FF00`, `#FFF` is `#FFFFFF`).
  - `#RRGGBBAA`: 8-digit form including Alpha (transparency). `AA` ranges from `00` (fully transparent) to `FF` (fully opaque). (e.g., `#0000FF80` is 50% transparent blue).
- **RGB / RGBA:** Specifies color using the Red, Green, Blue model, with values from 0 to 255. RGBA adds an Alpha channel for transparency (0 is fully transparent, 1 is fully opaque, decimals in between).
  - `rgb(R, G, B)`: e.g., `rgb(255, 0, 0)` is red.
  - `rgba(R, G, B, A)`: e.g., `rgba(0, 0, 255, 0.5)` is 50% transparent blue. You can also use percentages: `rgba(0%, 0%, 100%, 0.5)`.
- **HSL / HSLA:** Specifies color using Hue, Saturation, and Lightness. More intuitive for humans to understand color relationships than RGB. HSLA adds an Alpha channel.

o `hsl(H, S%, L%)`: Hue (0-360 degrees, representing colors around a wheel - 0/360 is red, 120 is green, 240 is blue), Saturation (0-100%, 0% is grayscale, 100% is full saturation), Lightness (0-100%, 0% is black, 100% is white, 50% is "pure" color). e.g., `hsl(0, 100%, 50%)` is red.

o `hsla(H, S%, L%, A)`: e.g., `hsla(240, 100%, 50%, 0.5)` is 50% transparent blue.

Personal Insight: While I used Hex for years, I find HSLA much more intuitive for picking and adjusting colors, especially for creating variations (like darkening or lightening a color). If you need a slightly darker shade of a color, in HSL you just decrease the Lightness value. In Hex/RGB, it's trial and error with the numbers. Plus, the Alpha channel in RGBA/HSLA is invaluable for subtle transparencies like semi-transparent overlays or text shadows.

6.4 Applying Colors to Elements and Backgrounds

Once you know how to specify colors, applying them is simple using the `color` and `background-color` properties.

`color`

- Sets the foreground color of an element's text and text decorations.

```css
p {
  color: #333; /* Dark gray text */
}


a {
  color: rgb(0, 123, 255); /* A blue link color */
}


.highlight {
  color: hsla(60, 100%, 50%, 0.8); /* Semi-transparent yellow text */
}
```

`background-color`

- Sets the solid background color of an element's content, padding, and border boxes (up to the border edge).

```css
.card {
  background-color: #f8f8f8; /* Light gray background */
}


button:hover {
```

```
  background-color: rgba(0, 0, 0, 0.1); /* Slightly transparent black
hover effect */
}
```

Color and Accessibility:

When choosing colors for text and backgrounds, always consider **color contrast**. People with visual impairments may struggle to read text if the contrast between the text color and its background color is too low. Web Content Accessibility Guidelines (WCAG) provide contrast ratios to aim for (4.5:1 for normal text, 3:1 for large text). There are many online tools to check contrast. Good contrast is crucial for a usable website for everyone.

6.5 Using Background Images and Gradients

Adding images or gradients as backgrounds can dramatically enhance visual appeal.

background-image

- Sets one or more background images for an element. You specify the path to the image file using `url()`.

```
.hero-section {
  background-image: url('images/background-photo.jpg'); /* Set a
background image */
}
```

Controlling Background Images:

Once you have a background image, you'll likely need to adjust how it behaves:

- **background-repeat**: Controls if/how the image repeats. `no-repeat` (show once), `repeat` (tile horizontally and vertically), `repeat-x` (tile horizontally), `repeat-y` (tile vertically).
- **background-position**: Sets the starting position of the background image within the element. Values can be keywords (`top`, `bottom`, `left`, `right`, `center`) or lengths/percentages (e.g., `background-position: center top;` or `background-position: 50% 50%;` for centering, `background-position: 20px 10px;`).
- **background-size**: Controls the size of the background image.
    - `auto` (default): Uses the image's natural size.
    - `cover`: Scales the image to be as large as possible while maintaining its aspect ratio, such that the background area is completely covered. Some parts of the image might be clipped. Ideal for hero sections.

- o   `contain`: Scales the image to be as large as possible while maintaining its aspect ratio, such that the image is fully visible within the background area. Empty space might appear. Ideal for logos or patterns.
    - o   Lengths/Percentages: e.g., `background-size: 200px auto;` (width 200px, height auto) or `background-size: 50% 100%;`.
- **`background-attachment`**: Determines whether the background image scrolls with the page or is fixed relative to the viewport.
    - o   `scroll` (default): Image scrolls with the element.
    - o   `fixed`: Image is fixed relative to the viewport, creating a parallax-like effect as the element scrolls over it.
    - o   `local`: Image scrolls with the element's content *within* the element (if the element itself has a scrollbar).

Shorthand `background`: Like `font`, `background` is a shorthand for many background properties (`background-image, background-position, background-size, background-repeat, background-origin, background-clip, background-attachment, background-color`). Order is flexible for most, but size must come after position, separated by a slash (/): `background-position / background-size`.

```
.hero-section {
  background: url('images/background-photo.jpg') no-repeat center
center / cover;
  /* This shorthand sets:
     image: url(...)
     repeat: no-repeat
     position: center center
     size: cover
  */
  background-color: #f0f0f0; /* A fallback color if image fails to
load */
  height: 400px; /* Give the section height to see the background */
}


.fixed-bg {
  background-image: url('images/parallax.jpg');
  background-attachment: fixed; /* Creates fixed background effect */
  background-position: center;
  background-size: cover;
  height: 500px;
}
```

Gradients (`linear-gradient`, `radial-gradient`)

Gradients are treated as a type of `<image>` in CSS and are created using functions like `linear-gradient()` and `radial-gradient()`. They are placed using the `background-image` property.

- **`linear-gradient()`**: Creates a gradient that transitions colors along a straight line.
  - Syntax: `linear-gradient(direction/angle, color-stop1, color-stop2, ...);`
  - Direction can be keywords (`to top`, `to right`, `to bottom right`) or an angle (`45deg`).
  - Color stops are the colors at specific points along the line.

```
.gradient-box {
  /* Gradient from top-left to bottom-right, blue to green */
  background-image: linear-gradient(to bottom right, blue, green);
  height: 100px;
}
```

```
.gradient-angled {
  /* Gradient at 90 degrees (left to right), with color stops at
specific points */
  background-image: linear-gradient(90deg, red 0%, yellow 50%, blue
100%);
  height: 100px;
}
```

- **`radial-gradient()`**: Creates a gradient that radiates outward from a central point.
  - Syntax: `radial-gradient(shape size at position, color-stop1, color-stop2, ...);`
  - Shape can be `circle` or `ellipse`. Size can be keywords (`closest-side, farthest-side, closest-corner, farthest-corner`) or lengths. Position is like `background-position`.

```
.radial-gradient-box {
  /* Radial gradient from center, circle shape, white to black */
  background-image: radial-gradient(circle at center, white, black);
  height: 100px;
}
```

6.6 Managing Multiple Backgrounds

A really cool feature is the ability to apply *multiple* background images (including gradients) to a single element. You list them, separated by commas, in the `background-image` (or `background`) property. The first image listed is the one closest to the user (on top), and the last one is furthest away (closest to the background color).

```
.layered-background {
  /* Multiple backgrounds, listed from top layer down */
  background-image: url('images/pattern.png'), /* Top layer: a pattern
*/
                    linear-gradient(to right, rgba(255,0,0,0.5),
rgba(0,0,255,0.5)), /* Middle layer: a semi-transparent gradient */
                    url('images/base-photo.jpg'); /* Bottom layer: a
photo */

  /* You can apply background properties layer by layer */
  background-repeat: repeat, /* pattern repeats */
                     no-repeat, /* gradient doesn't repeat */
                     no-repeat; /* photo doesn't repeat */

  background-position: top left, /* pattern positioned at top left */
                       center center, /* gradient centered */
                       center bottom; /* photo centered bottom */

  background-size: auto, /* pattern auto size */
                   100% 100%, /* gradient covers the element */
                   cover; /* photo covers the remaining area */

  background-color: #eee; /* Fallback solid color */
  height: 400px; /* Needs dimensions */
}
```

You can apply most `background-*` properties layer by layer by providing comma-separated values. The number of values should match the number of background images. If you provide fewer, the browser cycles through the list (e.g., if you have 3 images but only 2 `background-repeat` values, the third image will use the first repeat value).

Personal Insight: Using multiple backgrounds is fantastic for adding textures, overlays, or subtle effects without needing extra HTML elements just for decorative purposes. Combining a semi-transparent gradient overlay with a background image, for instance, is a great way to darken or colorize a photo to make overlying text more readable, and it's all handled cleanly in the CSS background property.

Chapter 6 Summary

You've now gained significant control over the visual presentation of your content:

- You learned how to control text appearance with **Typography** properties like `font-family`, `font-size`, `font-weight`, `font-style`, and the `font` shorthand.
- You understand the importance of using **Relative Units** like `rem` for font sizes and know how to include **Web Fonts** using `@font-face` or services like Google Fonts.
- You explored properties for **Styling Text Content** itself, including `text-align`, `text-decoration`, `text-transform`, `line-height`, and letter/word spacing.
- You're familiar with common **Color Models** like Hex, RGB(A), and HSL(A), and how to specify transparency.
- You know how to apply colors using `color` and `background-color`, remembering to consider **Accessibility** and contrast.
- You learned how to use **Background Images** with `url()` and control their behavior with `background-repeat`, `background-position`, `background-size`, and `background-attachment`.
- You can create **Gradients** using `linear-gradient()` and `radial-gradient()`.
- Finally, you discovered the power of applying **Multiple Backgrounds** to a single element.

These styling properties, combined with the layout techniques from previous chapters, give you the ability to create visually rich and engaging web pages. Practice applying different fonts, colors, and backgrounds to your existing layouts. Experiment with gradients and multiple backgrounds to see the effects!

Chapter 7: Adding Visual Interest: Transitions, Transforms, and Animations

Think about a well-designed mobile app or desktop software. Elements don't just instantly pop into existence or vanish. They often animate smoothly, maybe sliding into view, fading in, or subtly changing size or color. These small moments of motion provide visual feedback, make interfaces feel more responsive, and can simply delight the user.

CSS gives us powerful tools to add this kind of motion directly in our stylesheets, without needing JavaScript for simpler effects. This is often more performant because the browser can optimize these CSS-driven animations.

We'll cover three related but distinct concepts:

1. **Transitions:** Smooth changes from one CSS state to another over a duration.
2. **Transforms:** Geometrically altering an element's appearance (moving, rotating, scaling, skewing). These are often *what* you transition or animate.
3. **Animations:** More complex, multi-step sequences defined using `@keyframes` that can run automatically or on trigger.

Let's start with the simplest one.

7.1 Creating Smooth Property Changes with CSS Transitions

Imagine you have a button that changes color when you hover over it. By default, this change is instantaneous – SNAP! It just switches. A **CSS Transition** allows you to make that change happen smoothly over a specified duration. It handles the intermediate steps between the starting state and the ending state.

Transitions are perfect for animating changes that happen between two states, often triggered by user interaction (like hover, focus, or active) or by adding/removing a class with JavaScript.

You apply transition properties to the element in its *initial* state (the state *before* the change happens). This tells the browser, "When any of these properties *change* on this element, don't snap – transition them smoothly."

The main transition properties are:

- `transition-property`: Specifies which CSS property (or properties) to apply a transition to. Use `all` to transition any animatable property that changes.
- `transition-duration`: Defines how long the transition should take to complete. Measured in seconds (`s`) or milliseconds (`ms`). This is required for the transition to work!
- `transition-timing-function`: Describes how the intermediate values of the transition are calculated. This controls the *speed curve* of the animation (e.g., constant speed, speeding up, slowing down).

- **`transition-delay`**: Specifies a delay before the transition starts.

Let's make that button color change smooth:

```html
<!-- HTML -->
<button class="styled-button">Hover Over Me</button>
```

```css
/* CSS */
.styled-button {
  padding: 10px 20px;
  font-size: 16px;
  background-color: lightblue; /* Starting color */
  color: #333;
  border: none;
  border-radius: 5px;
  cursor: pointer;

  /* --- Transition Properties --- */
  /* Transition the 'background-color' property... */
  transition-property: background-color;
  /* ...over a duration of 0.3 seconds... */
  transition-duration: 0.3s;
  /* ...using a default easing function (ease) */
  transition-timing-function: ease;
  /* ...with no delay */
  transition-delay: 0s;

  /* You can transition multiple properties: */
  /* transition-property: background-color, color, transform; */
  /* Or transition ALL animatable properties (most common for simple
effects): */
  /* transition-property: all; */
}

/* The state the element transitions TO (e.g., on hover) */
.styled-button:hover {
  background-color: steelblue; /* Ending color */
  color: white; /* This property will NOT transition unless added to
transition-property */
```

```
    /* If transition-property was 'all', both background-color and color
    would transition */
}


/* You can also transition when a class is added/removed */
.styled-button.active {
    background-color: darkorange;
}
```

(Result: When you hover over the button, its background color smoothly changes from lightblue to steelblue over 0.3 seconds. When you hover off, it transitions smoothly back to lightblue.)

The `transition` Shorthand:

Just like `font` or `background`, there's a shorthand for transitions:

```
transition: [property] [duration] [timing-function] [delay];
```

Order for duration and delay matters: the first time value is duration, the second is delay.

```
.styled-button {
    /* ... other styles ... */

    /* Shorthand examples: */
    transition: background-color 0.3s ease; /* Common */
    /* Transition color and background-color, different durations */
    transition: color 0.2s ease-out, background-color 0.3s ease;
    /* Transition all properties over 0.5s */
    transition: all 0.5s ease;
}
```

Personal Insight: I almost always use the `transition: all [duration] [timing-function];` shorthand for simple effects like hover states. It's concise and means I don't have to remember to add every single property I might change. Just be mindful that transitioning "all" properties could potentially transition complex ones (like `box-shadow`) which can sometimes impact performance, though browsers are much better at optimizing this now. For performance-critical animations or complex components, specifying individual properties is better.

7.2 Transforming Elements in 2D and 3D Space (Translate, Rotate, Scale, Skew)

The `transform` property allows you to apply geometric transformations to an element without affecting the layout of other elements around it. Think of it as manipulating the element in place *after* the browser has determined its position and size in the normal flow.

Transforms are perfect candidates for *transitioning* or *animating*.

Common 2D transform functions:

- **`translate(x, y)`** : Moves the element. x is the horizontal shift, y is the vertical shift. Can use percentages (relative to the element's size) or lengths (px, em, etc.). `translateX(x)` and `translateY(y)` move only along one axis.
- **`rotate(angle)`** : Rotates the element around its origin. Angle is specified in degrees (`deg`), turns (`turn`), or radians (`rad`).
- **`scale(x, y)`** : Resizes the element. x is the horizontal scale factor, y is the vertical. `scale(value)` scales both equally. `scaleX(x)` and `scaleY(y)` scale only on one axis. Values less than 1 shrink, values greater than 1 enlarge.
- **`skew(angle-x, angle-y)`** : Skews the element along the X and Y axes. `skewX(angle)` and `skewY(angle)` skew only on one axis.

You can apply multiple transformations by listing them in the `transform` property, separated by spaces. The order matters!

```css
.box {
  width: 100px;
  height: 100px;
  background-color: lightcoral;
  margin: 50px; /* Add margin so transform doesn't overlap examples */
  transition: transform 0.3s ease; /* Add a transition for smooth
effect */
}

/* On hover, move the box, rotate it, and scale it */
.box:hover {
  /* First rotate, then translate, then scale */
  transform: rotate(10deg) translateX(20px) scale(1.1);
}

/* Example of combining transforms */
.icon {
```

```
    /* Move element up by 50% of its own height (useful for vertical
centering) */
    transform: translateY(-50%);
}


/* Example of skew */
.skewed-text {
    transform: skewX(10deg); /* Skew horizontally */
}
```

(Result: When hovering the box, it smoothly rotates 10 degrees, moves 20px to the right, and scales up by 10% simultaneously over 0.3 seconds.)

transform-origin

- Specifies the point around which a transform is applied. By default, transformations are applied from the center of the element (`50% 50%` or `center center`).
- Values can be keywords (`top`, `bottom`, `left`, `right`, `center`) or length/percentage values (e.g., `transform-origin: top left;` or `transform-origin: 0 0;`).

```
.rotate-from-corner {
    width: 50px;
    height: 50px;
    background-color: gold;
    margin: 50px;
    transition: transform 0.5s ease;
    transform-origin: 0 0; /* Set the origin to the top left corner */
}


.rotate-from-corner:hover {
    transform: rotate(90deg); /* Rotates around the top left corner */
}
```

(Result: The gold box rotates 90 degrees, pivoting specifically from its top-left corner, rather than its center.)

3D Transforms:

CSS also supports 3D transformations using functions like `translate3d(x, y, z)`, `rotateX(angle)`, `rotateY(angle)`, `rotateZ(angle)`, `scale3d(x, y, z)`, and `perspective(value)`. `perspective` is typically applied to the *container* of 3D elements to give them a sense of depth. 3D transforms are beyond the scope of a fundamentals chapter, but know they exist for more complex effects!

Personal Insight: Transforms are fantastic because they are very performant for animation. Browsers can often handle transforming elements on the GPU (Graphics Processing Unit) which is much faster than changing properties that affect the layout (like `width`, `height`, `margin`, or even `top`/`left` with `position: relative/absolute`). Whenever you can achieve a visual effect using `transform` (like movement or scaling) instead of layout properties, it's usually the better choice for performance.

7.3 Animating Elements with Keyframes

Transitions are great for simple A-to-B changes. But what if you need a sequence of changes, or an animation that loops, or one that starts automatically without a specific event like a hover? That's where **CSS Animations** and the `@keyframes` rule come in.

An animation consists of two parts:

1. The **@keyframes rule**: This is where you define the animation sequence. You give the animation a name and specify styles at different points in the animation's timeline (called "keyframes").
2. The **animation properties**: Applied to the element you want to animate, these properties tell the element *which* `@keyframes` animation to use, how long it should last, how many times to repeat, etc.

The @keyframes Rule:

You define this block anywhere in your CSS file (outside of any other rule).

```
/* Define an animation named 'fade-in' */
@keyframes fade-in {
  /* Keyframe at the start of the animation (0% or 'from') */
  0% {
    opacity: 0; /* Start completely transparent */
  }
  /* Keyframe at the end of the animation (100% or 'to') */
  100% {
    opacity: 1; /* End completely opaque */
  }
}


/* Define an animation named 'pulse' */
@keyframes pulse {
```

```
  0% {
    transform: scale(1); /* Start at normal size */
  }
  50% {
    transform: scale(1.05); /* At 50% mark, scale up slightly */
  }
  100% {
    transform: scale(1); /* Back to normal size at the end */
  }
}
```

- You define keyframes using percentage values (0% to 100%) or the keywords `from` (same as 0%) and `to` (same as 100%).
- You can define as many keyframes in between 0% and 100% as you need to create complex sequences.

Animation Properties (Applied to the element):

You apply these to the element you want to trigger the animation on.

- **animation-name**: The name of the `@keyframes` rule to use. (Required)
- **animation-duration**: How long one cycle of the animation takes. (Required)
- **animation-timing-function**: The speed curve for the animation (applies to the entire animation, though you can influence timing between keyframes).
- **animation-delay**: Delay before the animation starts.
- **animation-iteration-count**: How many times the animation should repeat. Can be a number (2, 5) or `infinite`.
- **animation-direction**: Whether the animation should play forwards, backwards, or alternate cycles. `normal` (default), `reverse`, `alternate`, `alternate-reverse`.
- **animation-fill-mode**: Specifies what styles the element should have *before* the animation starts and *after* it ends.
  - `none` (default): Styles are reset after the animation finishes.
  - `forwards`: Element retains the styles from the *last* keyframe (100% or `to`).
  - `backwards`: Element applies the styles from the *first* keyframe (0% or `from`) during the delay period, and keeps them after the animation finishes.
  - `both`: Applies both `forwards` and `backwards` behavior. (Often useful when you want the element to stay in its final state).
- **animation-play-state**: `running` (default) or `paused`. Useful for controlling animation with JavaScript (e.g., pausing an animation on hover).

```
/* Use the 'fade-in' animation on this element */
.fade-in-element {
```

```css
  /* Start the element hidden so the animation is visible */
  opacity: 0; /* Match the 0% keyframe */

  animation-name: fade-in;              /* Use the @keyframes fade-in */
  animation-duration: 1s;               /* Takes 1 second to complete */
  animation-timing-function: ease-out; /* Animation slows down towards
the end */
  animation-delay: 0.5s;                /* Wait 0.5 seconds before starting
*/
  animation-iteration-count: 1;     /* Play only once */
  animation-direction: normal;      /* Play forwards */
  animation-fill-mode: forwards;    /* Keep the final state (opacity:
1) after it ends */
}

/* Use the 'pulse' animation on this button */
.pulsing-button {
  padding: 10px 20px;
  background-color: dodgerblue;
  color: white;
  border: none;
  border-radius: 5px;

  animation-name: pulse;
  animation-duration: 2s;
  animation-timing-function: ease-in-out; /* Slow start and end, fast
in middle */
  animation-iteration-count: infinite; /* Repeat forever */
}
```

(Result: The `.fade-in-element` waits 0.5s, then fades smoothly from invisible to fully visible over 1 second, and stays visible. The `.pulsing-button` continuously scales slightly up and down every 2 seconds.)

The animation **Shorthand:**

Again, there's a shorthand, but the order is strict for duration and delay:

```css
animation: [name] [duration] [timing-function] [delay] [iteration-
count] [direction] [fill-mode] [play-state];
```

The first time value is duration, the second is delay. If only one time value, it's the duration.

```css
.fade-in-element {
  opacity: 0;
  animation: fade-in 1s ease-out 0.5s forwards; /* name | duration |
timing | delay | fill-mode */
  /* iteration-count is 1 (default), direction is normal (default),
play-state is running (default) */
}


.pulsing-button {
  animation: pulse 2s ease-in-out infinite; /* name | duration |
timing | iteration-count */
}
```

Personal Insight: @keyframes unlocked a new level of creativity for me in CSS. You can define complex sequences (like a bouncing ball, a multi-color flash, or elements appearing one after another) purely with CSS. Debugging complex animations can take patience – the "Animations" tab in browser developer tools is invaluable for inspecting and controlling running animations.

7.4 Controlling Animation Timing and Iteration

Let's look a bit closer at timing and repetition, as they are key to how an animation *feels*.

Timing Functions (transition-timing-function, animation-timing-function**)**

These define the acceleration curve of the animation between keyframes or between the start and end of a transition.

- ease (default): Slow start, fast middle, slow end.
- linear: Constant speed from start to end.
- ease-in: Slow start, speeds up towards the end.
- ease-out: Fast start, slows down towards the end.
- ease-in-out: Slow start and end, fast middle.
- cubic-bezier(x1, y1, x2, y2): Allows you to define a custom timing curve using specific points. Great for creating unique effects.
- steps(number, position): Divides the animation into a specific number of steps. The animation jumps between keyframes instead of transitioning smoothly. Useful for sprite sheet animations or digital counters. position is start or end (default).

Personal Insight: Playing with timing functions is a quick way to change the feel of an animation. `ease-in-out` often feels very smooth and natural. `linear` can feel mechanical. Custom `cubic-bezier` functions allow for unique bounces or accelerations if needed. Visual `cubic-bezier` generators are helpful tools!

Iteration Count and Direction (`animation-iteration-count, animation-direction`)

- `animation-iteration-count: infinite;` is powerful for creating continuous loops like loaders or background animations.
- `animation-direction: alternate;` is useful for animations that should play forwards then backwards. For example, a simple "move right" animation combined with `alternate` makes the element move right, then smoothly move back left.

Example:

```css
/* Define a simple left-right movement */
@keyframes slide {
  to { transform: translateX(100px); } /* Move 100px to the right */
}


.sliding-element {
  width: 50px;
  height: 50px;
  background-color: royalblue;
  animation-name: slide;
  animation-duration: 2s;
  animation-timing-function: linear; /* Constant speed */
  animation-iteration-count: infinite; /* Repeat forever */
  animation-direction: alternate; /* Play forwards, then backwards */
}
```

(Result: The box moves right for 2 seconds at a constant speed, then moves left for 2 seconds at a constant speed, repeating endlessly.)

7.5 Practical Examples of CSS Motion and Interactivity

Let's look at how we can combine these techniques for common interface elements.

Interactive Button with Transform and Transition:

Make a button slightly lift and scale on hover.

```css
.interactive-button {
  padding: 10px 20px;
  background-color: #007bff;
  color: white;
  border: none;
  border-radius: 5px;
  cursor: pointer;
  /* Add a subtle shadow for depth */
  box-shadow: 0 2px 5px rgba(0, 0, 0, 0.2);

  /* Transition ALL animatable properties */
  transition: all 0.2s ease-in-out;
}

.interactive-button:hover {
  /* Lift the button slightly (negative Y translate) */
  /* Scale it up a little */
  /* Darken the shadow */
  transform: translateY(-3px) scale(1.02);
  box-shadow: 0 5px 10px rgba(0, 0, 0, 0.3);
}

.interactive-button:active {
  /* When clicked, press it down */
  transform: translateY(0) scale(0.98);
  box-shadow: 0 2px 5px rgba(0, 0, 0, 0.2); /* Revert shadow */
}
```

(Result: The button smoothly lifts and scales when hovered, and presses down slightly when clicked.)

Fading/Sliding Modal or Notification:

Use @keyframes and animation-fill-mode to make an element appear smoothly.

```html
<!-- HTML (Initially hidden) -->
<div class="modal" id="myModal">
  <div class="modal-content">
    <span class="close-button">×</span>
```

```html
    <h2>Modal Title</h2>
    <p>This modal will fade and slide in.</p>
  </div>
</div>
```

```css
/* CSS */
.modal {
  position: fixed;
  top: 0;
  left: 0;
  width: 100%;
  height: 100%;
  background-color: rgba(0, 0, 0, 0.5); /* Semi-transparent overlay */
  display: flex; /* Use flexbox to center content */
  justify-content: center;
  align-items: center;
  opacity: 0; /* Start invisible */
  visibility: hidden; /* Hide completely from layout/interactions */
  transition: opacity 0.3s ease-out, visibility 0.3s ease-out; /*
Transition the overlay fade */
}

.modal-content {
  background-color: white;
  padding: 20px;
  border-radius: 8px;
  transform: translateY(50px); /* Start 50px below its final position
*/
  opacity: 0; /* Start invisible */
  /* No animation property here initially, we'll add it when shown */
}

/* State when the modal is visible (usually toggled by JS adding a
class) */
.modal.is-visible {
  opacity: 1;
  visibility: visible;
}
```

```css
/* Animation for the content when modal becomes visible */
.modal.is-visible .modal-content {
  animation-name: slide-up-fade-in;
  animation-duration: 0.5s;
  animation-timing-function: ease-out;
  animation-fill-mode: forwards; /* Stay in final state */
}

/* Define the animation */
@keyframes slide-up-fade-in {
  0% {
    opacity: 0;
    transform: translateY(50px); /* Match starting state in .modal-content */
  }
  100% {
    opacity: 1;
    transform: translateY(0); /* End at its final, untranslated position */
  }
}
```

(Result: When the `is-visible` *class is added to* `.modal`*, the background fades in smoothly. Simultaneously, the* `.modal-content` *element animates from 50px down and invisible to its normal position and fully visible, then stays there.)*

Personal Insight: Combining CSS animations (for the content entering) with CSS transitions (for the overlay fading) is a common and effective pattern for modals, sidebars, or other elements that appear and disappear. It keeps the JavaScript simple (just toggling a class) and lets CSS handle the smooth motion.

Chapter 7 Summary

You've added the exciting dimension of time and motion to your styling skills! You now understand:

- How **CSS Transitions** (`transition`) create smooth changes between two states of a property, often triggered by interactions like `:hover`.
- How **CSS Transforms** (`transform`) geometrically manipulate elements in 2D and 3D space (`translate`, `rotate`, `scale`, `skew`) without affecting layout, and how `transform-origin` controls the pivot point.

- How **CSS Animations** use `@keyframes` to define multi-step animation sequences.
- The key **Animation Properties** (`animation-name`, `animation-duration`, `animation-iteration-count`, `animation-direction`, `animation-fill-mode`, etc.) to control how and when `@keyframes` animations run on an element.
- The role of **Timing Functions** (`ease`, `linear`, `ease-in-out`, etc.) in controlling the speed curve of both transitions and animations.
- You've seen practical examples of how these techniques are used for interactive elements and visual effects.

Adding animation requires practice and experimentation. Use your browser's developer tools to inspect transitions and animations – they have dedicated panels that let you see the keyframes, adjust timing, and often visualize the timing function. Start with simple effects, then build up to more complex sequences. Remember to use animation and transitions thoughtfully to enhance the user experience, not distract from it!

Chapter 8: Advanced CSS Features

You've built a strong foundation: you understand syntax, selectors, the box model, layout with Flexbox and Grid, responsive design, and adding motion. You're already well on your way to building robust websites!

But CSS isn't a static language. It's constantly evolving, adding new features that address common development challenges and enable new design patterns. This chapter dives into some of these "advanced" features that, once you start using them, quickly become indispensable.

8.1 Using CSS Variables (Custom Properties) for Themability and Reusability

Have you ever worked on a project where you needed to use the same color value in dozens of different places? And then, when the client decides to change that primary brand color, you face the tedious task of finding and replacing that Hex or RGBA value everywhere? Or maybe you have a standard spacing value (like 1rem or 16px) that you use for margins and padding consistently, but want to easily tweak it globally?

This is exactly the problem that **CSS Variables** (officially called **Custom Properties**) solve! They allow you to define reusable values in your CSS, similar to variables in programming languages.

Defining a CSS Variable:

You define a custom property using two hyphens (--) followed by the variable name. You assign it a value like any other CSS property. Custom properties are subject to the cascade and inheritance, just like regular properties. The best place to define them for global use is often on the :root pseudo-class, which represents the <html> element.

```css
/* Define variables on the root element, making them globally
available */
:root {
  --primary-color: #007bff;        /* A brand blue */
  --secondary-color: #6c757d;      /* A gray */
  --spacing-unit: 1rem;            /* A standard spacing unit */
  --border-radius-small: 4px;      /* A small border radius */
  --box-shadow-subtle: 0 2px 5px rgba(0, 0, 0, 0.1); /* A reusable
shadow */
  --font-stack-body: 'Roboto', sans-serif; /* Even font stacks can be
variables */
}
```

Using a CSS Variable:

To use a custom property, you use the `var()` function, passing the variable name inside the parentheses.

```css
/* Use the defined variables */
body {
  font-family: var(--font-stack-body); /* Use the font stack variable
*/
}


.button {
  background-color: var(--primary-color); /* Use the primary color
variable */
  color: white;
  padding: var(--spacing-unit) calc(var(--spacing-unit) * 1.5); /* Use
spacing variable in calculation */
  border-radius: var(--border-radius-small);
  box-shadow: var(--box-shadow-subtle);
}


.button-secondary {
  background-color: var(--secondary-color); /* Use the secondary color
variable */
}


.card {
  margin-bottom: var(--spacing-unit); /* Use the spacing variable */
  border-radius: var(--border-radius-small);
  box-shadow: var(--box-shadow-subtle);
}
```

Benefits:

- **Reusability:** Define a value once, use it everywhere.
- **Maintainability:** To change a value (like the primary color), you only need to update it in one place (`:root`). This is incredibly powerful for theming!
- **Readability:** Variable names can be more semantic than raw values (e.g., `--primary-color` tells you more than `#007bff`).

- **Theming:** You can override variable values in different contexts (e.g., inside a `.dark-mode` class or a media query) to create themes or responsive adjustments easily.

Example of Theming:

```css
/* Define base colors */
:root {
  --bg-color: #fff;
  --text-color: #333;
  --accent-color: #007bff;
}

/* Default styles using variables */
body {
  background-color: var(--bg-color);
  color: var(--text-color);
}

.button {
  background-color: var(--accent-color);
  color: white;
}

/* Override variables for dark mode */
.dark-mode {
  --bg-color: #333; /* Dark background */
  --text-color: #f8f8f8; /* Light text */
  --accent-color: #66c2ff; /* Lighter accent */
}
```

Now, applying the `.dark-mode` class to your `<body>` or `<html>` element will automatically swap all styles using those variables!

Personal Insight: CSS variables are a game-changer. They bring real programming concepts into plain CSS, making large stylesheets much more manageable and flexible. I use them on almost every project now, primarily for colors, spacing, typography scales, and border radii. It makes refactoring styles or implementing design system changes dramatically faster.

8.2 Powerful CSS Functions: `calc()`, `min()`, `max()`, `clamp()`

CSS allows you to use functions to compute values dynamically. You've already seen `url()` for backgrounds and `var()` for custom properties. Here are some other incredibly useful mathematical and comparison functions:

`calc()`

- Allows you to perform simple mathematical operations (addition +, subtraction -, multiplication *, division /) to determine a CSS property value. You can mix different units (e.g., pixels and percentages).
- **Important:** You *must* have spaces around the + and - operators. Spaces around * and / are optional but recommended for readability.

```css
.sidebar {
  /* Make the sidebar 200px wide, PLUS 10px padding on each side */
  width: calc(200px + 20px);
  /* Or make it a percentage minus a fixed value */
  width: calc(30% - 20px); /* 30% of parent width, minus 20px */
}


.header {
  /* Make header height equal to content height + top/bottom padding */
  padding: 10px 20px;
  height: calc(50px + 20px); /* Content is 50px + 10px top + 10px
bottom padding */
}


.full-height-minus-header {
  /* Make this element take up full viewport height minus the header's
height */
  height: calc(100vh - 60px); /* Assuming header is 60px tall */
}


.button {
  padding: var(--spacing-unit) calc(var(--spacing-unit) * 1.5); /*
Using calc with variables */
}
```

- **Use case:** Calculating dimensions or offsets based on combinations of units, like taking up remaining space, setting padding relative to width, or accounting for fixed headers/footers.

`min()`, `max()`, and `clamp()`

These functions are fantastic for creating fluid and responsive designs by setting a value that's constrained within a range or chooses between options.

- **`min(value1, value2, ...)`**: Sets the property value to the *smallest* value from a list of comma-separated values.
    - Example: `width: min(500px, 50%);` The element's width will be 50% of its container *or* 500px, whichever is *smaller*. This prevents a fluid element from becoming too wide on large screens.
- **`max(value1, value2, ...)`**: Sets the property value to the *largest* value from a list of comma-separated values.
    - Example: `width: max(200px, 50%);` The element's width will be 50% of its container *or* 200px, whichever is *larger*. This prevents a fluid element from becoming too narrow on small screens.
- **`clamp(min, preferred, max)`**: This is a combination of `min()` and `max()` and is excellent for fluid typography or fluid spacing. It sets a value that stays within a minimum and maximum boundary but scales based on a "preferred" value in between.
    - `min`: The minimum possible value (e.g., `1rem`).
    - `preferred`: The value that is used if it's between `min` and `max`. This is often a value based on a relative unit like `vw` or a `calc()` expression (e.g., `2vw + 0.5rem`).
    - `max`: The maximum possible value (e.g., `2rem`).
    - Example: `font-size: clamp(1rem, 2vw + 0.5rem, 2rem);` The font size will never be smaller than 1rem or larger than 2rem, but in between, it will scale dynamically based on the viewport width.

Personal Insight: `min()`, `max()`, and especially `clamp()` are modern power tools for responsive design. They allow you to create truly fluid, elegant scaling for font sizes, padding, margins, and widths without relying on as many explicit media query breakpoints. It's a more natural, continuous way to handle responsiveness.

8.3 Exploring Newer Selectors and Pseudo-classes

(`:is()`, `:where()`, `:has()`, `:not()`)
CSS Selectors are constantly being refined to give you more power and flexibility in targeting elements. While Type, Class, and ID selectors are the bread and butter, newer pseudo-classes offer more advanced ways to select elements based on their state, position, or even their content (with `:has()`).

- **`:not(selector)`**: Excludes elements that match the given selector.
    - Example: `div:not(.promo) { ... }` - Selects all `div` elements EXCEPT those with the class `.promo`.

- o Example: `a:not(:last-child) { margin-right: 10px; }` - Adds right margin to all links EXCEPT the last one. (Useful for spacing lists/navs).
- `:is(selector-list)`: Matches any element that matches *any* selector in the comma-separated list. It's a powerful way to group selectors and reduce repetition. Specificity-wise, `:is()` takes the specificity of its *most specific* argument.
  - o Example: `h1:is(.large, .small) { color: blue; }` is the same as `h1.large, h1.small { color: blue; }`.
  - o Example: `:is(h1, h2, h3):hover { text-decoration: underline; }` - Underlines any h1, h2, or h3 on hover. Much shorter than `h1:hover, h2:hover, h3:hover`.
- `:where(selector-list)`: Works exactly like `:is()`, matching any element that matches any selector in the list. The key difference is that `:where()` *always* has **zero specificity**. This makes it useful for creating reusable helper styles that can be easily overridden.
  - o Example: `:where(.button, .link) { cursor: pointer; }` - Sets cursor for elements with class `.button` or `.link`. Because `:where` has zero specificity, a simple rule like `.button { cursor: default; }` elsewhere in your CSS can easily override it.
- `:has(selector-list)`: (Often called the "Parent Selector" or "Container Query Selector" though it's more flexible). This pseudo-class is applied to a subject selector and selects that subject *only if* it contains an element matching one of the selectors in the list. This allows you to style an element based on its *descendants*. Support for `:has()` is excellent in modern browsers but might require checking if targeting older ones.
  - o Example: `section:has(h1) { border-top: 2px solid red; }` - Selects a `section` element *only if* it contains an `h1` element somewhere inside it.
  - o Example: `label:has(+ input:checked) { font-weight: bold; }` - Selects a `label` *only if* it is immediately followed by a checked input (useful for styling form labels based on input state).
  - o Example: `.card:has(img) { padding: 0; }` - Selects a `.card` *only if* it contains an image, perhaps to remove padding around the image.

Personal Insight: `:is()` and `:where()` are great for tidying up repetitive selector lists. But `:has()` is truly revolutionary! For years, we couldn't select a parent based on its child in CSS, often resorting to JavaScript. `:has()` unlocks powerful new styling patterns based on content relationships. I'm excited to see how it gets used as browser support becomes universal.

8.4 Understanding CSS Blend Modes and Filters

These features, often borrowed from graphic design software, allow you to manipulate the appearance of elements visually.

filter()

- Applies graphical effects to an element before it is displayed. These are often used for adjusting images or adding visual flair.
- Values are functions like:
  - `blur(radius)`: Blurs the element.
  - `brightness(value)`: Adjusts brightness (1 is normal).
  - `contrast(value)`: Adjusts contrast (1 is normal).
  - `grayscale(%)`: Converts to grayscale.
  - `hue-rotate(angle)`: Shifts the hues.
  - `invert(%)`: Inverts colors.
  - `opacity(value)`: Adjusts transparency (0 to 1). (Similar to the `opacity` property, but as a filter).
  - `sepia(%)`: Converts to sepia.
  - `saturate(value)`: Adjusts saturation (1 is normal).
  - `drop-shadow(offset-x offset-y blur-radius spread-radius color)`: Adds a drop shadow (similar to `box-shadow` but applied to the shape of the element's content, not just its box).

You can apply multiple filters by listing them in the `filter` property, separated by spaces.

```css
img {
  filter: grayscale(100%); /* Make all images grayscale by default */
  transition: filter 0.3s ease; /* Transition the filter effect */
}


img:hover {
  filter: grayscale(0%) brightness(1.1); /* Remove grayscale and
increase brightness on hover */
}


.blurred-background {
  /* Apply a blur filter (often used with pseudo-elements or layered
images) */
  filter: blur(5px);
}


.icon-with-shadow {
  filter: drop-shadow(3px 3px 2px rgba(0, 0, 0, 0.5)); /* Add a shadow
that follows the icon shape */
}
```

(Result: Images are initially black and white, but smoothly transition to full color and slightly brighter on hover. The icon gets a shadow that wraps around its non-rectangular shape.)

`mix-blend-mode` and `background-blend-mode`

- These properties specify how an element's content (`mix-blend-mode`) or background images/gradients (`background-blend-mode`) should blend with the content stack below it.
- Values include standard blending modes like `multiply, screen, overlay, darken, lighten, color-dodge, color-burn, hard-light, soft-light, difference, exclusion, hue, saturation, color, luminosity`.

Example (requires overlapping elements or stacked backgrounds):

```html
<!-- HTML -->
<div class="blend-container">
  <div class="blend-element">
    <h2>Overlay Text</h2>
  </div>
</div>
```

```css
/* CSS */
.blend-container {
  position: relative; /* Establish positioning context */
  width: 300px;
  height: 200px;
  background: url('images/colorful-photo.jpg') center / cover no-repeat; /* Background image */
}

.blend-element {
  position: absolute; /* Position over the background */
  top: 0;
  left: 0;
  width: 100%;
  height: 100%;
  background-color: #00f; /* A blue background */
  /* Blend the blue background with the photo below it */
  mix-blend-mode: overlay; /* Try 'multiply', 'screen', etc. */
  display: flex; /* Center text */
  justify-content: center;
```

```
    align-items: center;
}


.blend-element h2 {
  color: white;
}
```

(Result: The blue background of `.blend-element` is blended with the background image of its parent using the 'overlay' mode, creating a colorful, potentially stylized effect over the photo. The white text inside the blend element remains unaffected by the blending mode.)

Personal Insight: Blend modes and filters are fantastic for creating visually rich effects that previously required image editing software. They open up a lot of creative possibilities for backgrounds, images, and text effects directly in the browser. Like animations, they are generally performant as they leverage the GPU.

Chapter 8 Summary

You've ventured into the more advanced capabilities of modern CSS:

- You learned the power of **CSS Variables (`--property: value;`)** and the **`var()`** function for creating reusable, maintainable, and themeable styles.
- You explored powerful **CSS Functions** like `calc()` for calculations and `min()`, `max()`, `clamp()` for creating fluid and constrained values.
- You were introduced to newer **Selectors and Pseudo-classes** like `:is()`, `:where()` (for grouping), and the game-changing `:has()` (for selecting based on content).
- You saw how **CSS Filters** (`filter()`) can apply graphical effects to elements.
- You learned about **CSS Blend Modes** (`mix-blend-mode`, `background-blend-mode`) for combining the colors of overlapping elements or backgrounds.

These features allow you to write more dynamic, less repetitive, and visually richer CSS. They might take a little getting used to, but the benefits in terms of maintainability, flexibility, and creative control are immense. Practice integrating CSS variables into your projects and experimenting with the functions and visual effects.

Chapter 9: Working with External Tools and Methodologies

You've built a solid foundation with core CSS, mastered modern layout with Flexbox and Grid, made your sites responsive, styled text and backgrounds, and even added motion. You're ready to build real things!

As you start working on larger projects, perhaps collaborating with other developers or building complex design systems, you'll quickly run into the limitations of just writing CSS rules in one big file (or even multiple files linked traditionally). You might find yourself repeating color values, writing long chains of selectors, or struggling to keep class names unique.

This chapter introduces various approaches and tools from the wider CSS ecosystem that help solve these problems. They don't replace CSS itself, but they provide extra features, structures, or ways of thinking that make writing and managing CSS at scale much more efficient.

9.1 Introduction to CSS Preprocessors (Sass, Less): Variables, Nesting, Mixins

Imagine writing CSS with superpowers – features like variables, the ability to nest your rules visually like your HTML structure, creating reusable blocks of styles, and even doing simple math. That's what CSS preprocessors offer!

A preprocessor is essentially a scripting language that extends CSS. You write your styles using the preprocessor's syntax (e.g., `.scss` files for Sass, `.less` files for Less), and then you use a preprocessor tool (usually via your project's build process, like Webpack, Parcel, or a dedicated task runner) to compile that code into standard, browser-readable `.css` files.

Sass (Syntactically Awesome Style Sheets) and Less (Leaner Style Sheets) are the two most popular preprocessors. They share many similar features, but Sass (specifically the SCSS syntax, which is a superset of CSS – meaning valid CSS is also valid SCSS) is currently the most widely used. We'll focus on SCSS syntax for examples, but the concepts apply to Less too.

Let's look at some key features:

Variables:

Unlike native CSS variables (Custom Properties) which are dynamic and can be changed at runtime in the browser, preprocessor variables are defined at *compile time*. They are great for storing reusable values like colors, fonts, or spacing before the CSS is generated.

```
/* SCSS Syntax (using Sass) */
$primary-color: #3498db; // Define a variable with $
$font-stack: 'Helvetica Neue', sans-serif;
$base-spacing: 16px;
```

```scss
body {
  font-family: $font-stack; // Use the variable
  line-height: 1.5;
}

.button {
  background-color: $primary-color;
  padding: $base-spacing / 2 $base-spacing; // Use variables in
calculations
  border: none;
  border-radius: 4px;
}

/* Compiled CSS Output */
body {
  font-family: 'Helvetica Neue', sans-serif;
  line-height: 1.5;
}

.button {
  background-color: #3498db;
  padding: 8px 16px;
  border: none;
  border-radius: 4px;
}
```

Comparison to CSS Variables: Preprocessor variables are useful during development for defining constants. Native CSS variables are dynamic, can be changed with JavaScript or media queries, and are subject to the cascade, making them better for runtime theming and dynamic values. You can, and often do, use *both* – define core values in preprocessor variables, then assign them to CSS variables for runtime flexibility (`--primary-color: $brand-blue;`).

Nesting:

Preprocessors allow you to nest CSS selectors inside one another, mirroring the structure of your HTML. This can make your CSS feel more organized and reduce repetition, but it needs to be used carefully to avoid overly long and specific selectors.

```scss
/* SCSS Syntax */
```

```scss
.card {
  border: 1px solid #ccc;
  padding: 15px;

  h3 { // Styles for h3 ONLY inside a .card
    color: #333;
    margin-bottom: 10px;
  }

  .button { // Styles for elements with class .button ONLY inside a
.card
    background-color: $primary-color; // Using the variable from above
    padding: 8px 12px;

    &:hover { // Styles for .button:hover ONLY inside a .card (&
refers to the parent selector)
      background-color: darken($primary-color, 10%); // Example
preprocessor function
    }
  }
}

/* Compiled CSS Output */
.card {
  border: 1px solid #ccc;
  padding: 15px;
}

.card h3 { /* Compiled nested selector */
  color: #333;
  margin-bottom: 10px;
}

.card .button { /* Compiled nested selector */
  background-color: #3498db;
  padding: 8px 12px;
}

.card .button:hover { /* Compiled nested selector using & */
```

```
    background-color: #2980b9; /* Result of darken function */
}
```

Personal Insight: Nesting can be a double-edged sword. It makes reading the source SCSS/Less match the HTML structure which feels nice initially. However, over-nesting quickly leads to extremely high selector specificity (`.parent .child .grandchild button`) which is difficult to override later and contributes to CSS bloat. I've learned to use nesting sparingly, usually only 1 or 2 levels deep, primarily for component elements or state changes (`.button:hover, .button--disabled`).

Mixins:

Mixins are reusable blocks of CSS declarations that you can include in multiple rules. This is fantastic for avoiding repetition of common code patterns, like vendor prefixes for older browsers or complex sets of declarations (like a button reset).

```scss
/* SCSS Syntax */
@mixin button-base { // Define a mixin
  display: inline-block;
  padding: 10px 15px;
  border-radius: 5px;
  cursor: pointer;
  text-align: center;
}

@mixin themed-button($bg-color, $text-color: white) { // Mixins can
accept arguments
  @include button-base; // Include another mixin
  background-color: $bg-color;
  color: $text-color;
  border: 1px solid darken($bg-color, 10%);
}

.primary-button {
  @include themed-button($primary-color); // Include the mixin,
passing the color variable
}

.secondary-button {
```

```
  @include themed-button(#ccc, #333); // Include with different
arguments
}

/* Compiled CSS Output */
.primary-button {
  display: inline-block;
  padding: 10px 15px;
  border-radius: 5px;
  cursor: pointer;
  text-align: center;
  background-color: #3498db;
  color: white;
  border: 1px solid #2980b9;
}

.secondary-button {
  display: inline-block;
  padding: 10px 15px;
  border-radius: 5px;
  cursor: pointer;
  text-align: center;
  background-color: #ccc;
  color: #333;
  border: 1px solid #b3b3b3;
}
```

Personal Insight: Mixins are invaluable for patterns that repeat often. I use them extensively for things like flexbox centering (`@mixin flex-center { display: flex; justify-content: center; align-items: center; }`), clearing floats (though less needed now), and applying consistent visual effects like shadows or transitions across different components.

Other Preprocessor Features:

- **Partials and Imports:** Break your SCSS/Less into smaller, manageable files (partials, starting with _, like `_variables.scss`) and import them into a main file (`@import 'variables';`). The compiler merges them into a single output CSS file. Essential for organizing large projects.

- **Functions:** Perform operations that return a value
  (like `darken()`, `lighten()`, `percentage()`).
- **Operators:** Perform mathematical operations directly on values (like +, -, *, /) which is useful in `calc()` or for calculating dimensions.

Preprocessors are powerful tools for developers comfortable with a build step, offering significant benefits in terms of organization and features compared to vanilla CSS (though native CSS is catching up with variables, and nesting is being standardized).

9.2 Organizing CSS with Methodologies (BEM, OOCSS, SMACSS)

While preprocessors offer syntax features, methodologies provide strategic guidance on *how* to structure and name your CSS to keep it maintainable and scalable over time, especially in teams. They are often used *alongside* preprocessors or even modern techniques like CSS Modules.

The core problem they address is the global nature of CSS: how do you prevent styles for one component from accidentally affecting another, and how do you make it clear what a CSS rule is intended for?

Let's briefly look at some prominent methodologies:

`BEM (Block, Element, Modifier):`

Focuses on a strict naming convention to make it obvious what a CSS class does and its relationship to other classes.

- **Block:** A standalone component or section (e.g., `.button`, `.card`, `.header`).
- **Element:** A part of a Block that has no standalone meaning
  (e.g., `.card__title`, `.button__icon`). Separated by two underscores (`__`).
- **Modifier:** A flag on a Block or Element to change its appearance or behavior
  (e.g., `.button--primary`, `.card--featured`, `.button__icon--large`).
  Separated by two hyphens (`--`).

```html
<!-- Example BEM HTML -->
<div class="card">
  <h3 class="card__title">Card Title</h3>
  <p class="card__text">Card content.</p>
  <button class="button button--primary">Learn More</button>
  <button class="button button--secondary">Dismiss</button>
</div>


<button class="button button--primary button--large">Large Primary
Button</button>
```

```css
/* Example BEM CSS */
.card { /* Block */
  border: 1px solid #ccc;
}

.card__title { /* Element of Card */
  font-size: 1.2em;
}

.button { /* Block */
  display: inline-block;
  padding: 10px 15px;
}

.button--primary { /* Modifier of Button */
  background-color: blue;
  color: white;
}

.button--secondary { /* Modifier of Button */
  background-color: gray;
}

.button--large { /* Another Modifier of Button */
  padding: 15px 25px;
  font-size: 1.1em;
}
```

Personal Insight: BEM's naming convention is opinionated and can lead to long class names, but it's incredibly effective at signaling intent and managing specificity. A BEM class like .card__title is much more specific than just .title, reducing naming collisions. It enforces a discipline that pays off in larger codebases. It was one of the first methodologies I adopted seriously, and it significantly improved the clarity of my CSS.

OOCSS (Object-Oriented CSS):
Based on two main principles:

1. **Separate structure and skin:** Create abstract objects (like a `.media-object` for an image next to content) that handle layout (`structure`), and then apply visual styles (`skin`) separately (`.blue`, `.rounded`).

2. **Separate container and content:** Styles for an object should not be dependent on where it's placed (its container). An object should look the same whether it's in a sidebar or the main content area. Avoid location-dependent selectors like `.sidebar .widget`.

```html
<!-- Example OOCSS HTML (simplified) -->
<div class="media-object flag"> <!-- Structure classes -->
  <img src="..." alt="..." class="media-object__img">
  <div class="media-object__body">
    Content here.
  </div>
</div>


<button class="btn blue large"> <!-- Structure and Skin/Size classes -->
  Click Me
</button>


/* Example OOCSS CSS (simplified) */
/* Structure */
.media-object { overflow: hidden; }
.media-object__img { float: left; margin-right: 10px; } /* Or use Flexbox/Grid */
.media-object__body { overflow: hidden; }

/* Skin (could be applied anywhere) */
.blue { background-color: blue; color: white; }
.rounded { border-radius: 5px; }

/* Size (could be applied anywhere) */
.large { font-size: 1.2em; padding: 15px; }
```

OOCSS emphasizes creating reusable "objects" (like BEM blocks) and applying visual styles and behaviors via modifier classes, keeping the base object styles purely structural.

SMACSS (Scalable and Modular Architecture for CSS):
Provides a way to categorize CSS rules into five types:

1. **Base:** Default styles for HTML elements (e.g., `body, h1, a {}`).
2. **Layout:** Styles for major page regions or grid systems
   (e.g., `#header, .sidebar, .grid-container {}`). Often prefixed
   with `l-` or `layout-`.
3. **Module:** Reusable, modular components (like BEM blocks/OOCSS objects)
   (e.g., `.card, .button, .modal {}`).
4. **State:** Styles describing the state of an element or layout (e.g., `.is-active, .is-`
   `hidden, .button.is-disabled {}`). Often prefixed with `is-`.
5. **Theme:** Styles for visual themes (colors, images) that override base/module styles
   (e.g., `.theme-dark {}`).

SMACSS provides a clear structure for organizing your CSS files and thinking about the role of different styles.

Personal Insight: Methodologies like BEM and SMACSS force you to be more intentional about how you name and organize your CSS. This discipline pays off hugely in larger projects by preventing chaos and making it easier for team members to understand and contribute to the stylesheet. You don't have to follow any methodology religiously, but adopting some of their core principles (like consistent naming and separating concerns) is highly recommended.

9.3 CSS Modules: Scoped Styling

We covered this in detail in Chapter X. CSS Modules offer a tooling-based approach to the global scope problem. Instead of relying on manual naming conventions (like BEM) or complex selector chains to achieve isolation, your build process automatically transforms class names to be unique and scoped to specific component files.

- **Key takeaway:** When you write `.my-class` in `Component.module.css` and import it
  into `Component.js`, the build tool generates a unique name like `Component_my-`
  `class_abc12` and provides that unique name via a JavaScript object
  (`styles.myClass`). This guarantees that `.my-class` defined *only* in that module
  won't conflict with a `.my-class` defined anywhere else.
- **Benefit:** Eliminates naming collisions and makes components' styles truly encapsulated.
- **Often used with:** Component-based JavaScript frameworks like React, Vue, or Angular,
  as the build setup is typically integrated.

CSS Modules are a modern alternative or complement to manual methodologies for solving the naming/scoping problem at the component level.

9.4 A Brief Look at Utility-First CSS (Tailwind CSS) and Component Libraries

Finally, let's touch upon two other significant approaches to managing CSS, which represent different philosophies.

Utility-First CSS (e.g., Tailwind CSS):

Instead of writing semantic class names like `.card` or `.button--primary` that represent a component, utility-first frameworks provide a large set of low-level, single-purpose classes that you compose directly in your HTML.

Think of classes like:

- `flex`, `items-center`, `justify-center` (Flexbox utilities)
- `grid`, `grid-cols-3`, `gap-4` (Grid utilities)
- `pt-4`, `pb-6`, `mx-auto` (Padding/Margin utilities)
- `text-xl`, `font-bold`, `text-blue-500` (Typography/Color utilities)
- `shadow-md`, `rounded-lg` (Visual utilities)

You build components by stringing these classes together in your HTML:

```html
<!-- Example Tailwind CSS HTML -->
<div class="flex items-center justify-center h-screen bg-gray-100">
<!-- Centers the card in the viewport -->
  <div class="bg-white p-6 rounded-lg shadow-xl max-w-sm w-full"> <!--
Card styling -->
    <h2 class="text-2xl font-bold mb-2">Welcome</h2>
    <p class="text-gray-700">This is a utility-first example.</p>
    <button class="mt-4 bg-blue-500 text-white px-4 py-2 rounded
hover:bg-blue-600">
      Click Me
    </button>
  </div>
</div>
```

Personal Insight: Utility-first, spearheaded by Tailwind CSS, has become incredibly popular. The promise is rapid development and eliminating the "naming problem" entirely because you're not inventing new class names. The HTML can look busy, but the styles are local to the component markup. It's a different way of thinking about the separation of concerns (styling is separated from CSS files, but less separated from HTML markup). I find it very fast for prototyping and building standard UI elements, though complex or unique designs can sometimes still require custom CSS.

Component Libraries (e.g., Bootstrap, Materialize, Ant Design):

These frameworks provide pre-designed and pre-coded UI components (buttons, forms, navigation bars, modals, grids, etc.) that you can drop into your project. They typically include their own CSS (often based on a grid system and predefined components), and sometimes JavaScript.

You use them by adding specific classes to your HTML elements, often following their documentation.

```html
<!-- Example Bootstrap HTML -->
<div class="container"> <!-- Responsive container -->
  <div class="row"> <!-- Row for grid -->
    <div class="col-sm-6 col-md-4"> <!-- Responsive column classes -->
      <div class="card"> <!-- Card component -->
        <div class="card-body">
          <h5 class="card-title">Card Title</h5>
          <p class="card-text">Some quick example text...</p>
          <a href="#" class="btn btn-primary">Go somewhere</a> <!--
Button component classes -->
        </div>
      </div>
    </div>
    <!-- More columns here -->
  </div>
</div>
```

Personal Insight: Component libraries like Bootstrap are fantastic for quickly building standard interfaces or getting a project off the ground fast. They provide consistency and often handle complex things like responsiveness and accessibility out-of-the-box. The trade-off is that customization can sometimes be tricky, and sites built with the default styles can look similar. Many modern libraries are becoming more modular or themeable to address this.

Chapter 9 Summary

Managing CSS effectively is crucial for projects of any significant size. You've explored several approaches and tools that help:

- **CSS Preprocessors (Sass, Less)** extend CSS with features like variables (compile-time), nesting, mixins, and imports, compiled down to standard CSS.
- **CSS Methodologies (BEM, OOCSS, SMACSS)** provide structural guidelines and naming conventions to organize and maintain CSS code, tackling the global scope problem manually.
- **CSS Modules** (covered in detail previously) offer a tooling-based solution for automatic local scope, particularly relevant in component-based frameworks.

- **Utility-First CSS (Tailwind)** provides low-level, single-purpose classes composed directly in HTML for rapid styling.
- **Component Libraries (Bootstrap, etc.)** offer pre-built UI components with included CSS and sometimes JavaScript for accelerated development and consistency.

None of these approaches are mutually exclusive, and there's no single "best" way. Many projects combine them – using a preprocessor *with* BEM naming, or using CSS Modules *with* some core variables defined in native CSS, or using a utility framework for layout *within* components styled with more semantic CSS. The choice depends on the project's needs, the team's preferences, and the existing tech stack.

The important thing is to be aware of these options and understand the problems they solve. As you gain more experience, you'll develop your own preferences and perhaps even combine ideas from different approaches to find what works best for you and your team.

With the foundational CSS concepts and layout techniques covered, and now an understanding of how to manage them at scale, you have the knowledge to build a vast range of web interfaces. In the next chapter, we'll put all these pieces together by building complete, practical projects!

Chapter 10: Building Real-World Projects

Welcome to the practical playground! You've armed yourself with the fundamental building blocks, the powerful layout tools, the secrets of responsiveness, and the art of styling and motion. Now, let's put those weapons to use and craft some common, real-world web components and layouts.

The projects in this chapter are designed to combine the concepts from previous chapters. We'll start with a base HTML structure for each, and then layer on the CSS step-by-step, focusing on the modern techniques we've discussed. Remember our mobile-first philosophy as we build!

10.1 Project 1: Developing a Responsive Navigation Bar

A navigation bar is one of the most common elements on any website. On a wide screen, you typically see a horizontal row of links. On a narrow screen (like a phone), this needs to collapse into a compact format, often a single column stack or a "hamburger" menu that toggles visibility. We'll build the core horizontal layout and then make it responsive.

Goal: Create a navigation bar that displays horizontally on desktop and stacks vertically on mobile.

Concepts Reinforced: Flexbox (`display`, `justify-content`), Basic Styling (`padding`, `background-color`, `text-decoration`), Media Queries (`min-width`), Box Model.

HTML Structure:

We'll use a `nav` element as our container, and an unordered list (`ul`) with list items (`li`) containing anchor tags (`a`) for the links.

```html
<!-- Inside your body tag -->
<nav class="navbar">
  <ul class="navbar-list">
    <li class="navbar-item"><a href="#" class="navbar-
link">Home</a></li>
    <li class="navbar-item"><a href="#" class="navbar-
link">About</a></li>
    <li class="navbar-item"><a href="#" class="navbar-
link">Services</a></li>
    <li class="navbar-item"><a href="#" class="navbar-
link">Contact</a></li>
  </ul>
</nav>
```

```html
<!-- Add some content below the nav so you can scroll if needed -->
<div style="height: 100vh; background-color: #f0f0f0; padding: 20px;">
  <h2>Scrollable Content Below</h2>
  <p>Add enough content here to make the page scroll if you want to
test sticky or fixed headers later.</p>
</div>
```

CSS Implementation (Step-by-Step):
Step 1: Base Styles (Mobile-First)

We start with the mobile view. By default, `li` elements are block-level, so they'll stack vertically. We'll add some basic styling to the nav container and links.

```css
/* --- Project 1: Responsive Navigation Bar --- */

/* Basic reset for list */
.navbar-list {
  list-style: none; /* Remove bullets */
  padding: 0;       /* Remove default padding */
  margin: 0;        /* Remove default margin */
}

/* Nav container styling */
.navbar {
  background-color: #333; /* Dark background */
  padding: 10px 20px;     /* Add some padding */
}

/* Nav item styling (mobile: stacked) */
.navbar-item {
  margin-bottom: 10px; /* Add space between stacked items */
}

/* Nav link styling */
.navbar-link {
  display: block; /* Make links fill the item width for easier
clicking */
  color: white;
```

```
  text-decoration: none; /* Remove underline */
  padding: 8px 0;        /* Add vertical padding */
  transition: color 0.3s ease; /* Smooth color change on hover */
}


.navbar-link:hover {
  color: #007bff; /* Change color on hover */
}
```

(Result: On all screen sizes, you'll see a dark gray bar with white links stacked vertically, each with a bottom margin.)

Step 2: Desktop Layout with Flexbox

Now, let's make it horizontal for wider screens. We'll use a media query and Flexbox on the `.navbar-list`.

```
/* Add this *after* the base styles */

/* Media query for larger screens (e.g., 600px and up) */
@media (min-width: 600px) {
  .navbar-list {
    display: flex; /* Turn the list into a flex container */
    justify-content: center; /* Center the links horizontally */
    align-items: center;   /* Vertically center items (if they had
different heights) */
  }

  .navbar-item {
    /* Remove mobile margin-bottom */
    margin-bottom: 0;
    /* Add margin-right instead for horizontal spacing */
    margin-right: 20px;
  }

  /* Remove margin-right from the last item to prevent trailing space
*/
  .navbar-item:last-child {
    margin-right: 0;
```

```
  }

  .navbar-link {
    /* Revert display if you don't want them to fill item width
horizontally */
    /* display: inline-block; */
    padding: 0 10px; /* Adjust padding for horizontal links */
  }
}
```

(Result: Below 600px, the links stack. At 600px and wider, the `ul` becomes a flex container, arranging the list items horizontally in the center, with space between them. The `margin-bottom` is removed, and `margin-right` is added.)

Step 3: Optional - Adding a Border Separator

Instead of margin, you could add a border between items for a different look.

```
/* Modify the media query from Step 2 */
@media (min-width: 600px) {
  .navbar-list {
    display: flex;
    justify-content: center;
    align-items: center;
    /* Remove margin-right from items if using borders */
    /* margin-right: 0; */
  }

  .navbar-item {
    margin-bottom: 0; /* Still remove this */
    /* If using borders, remove margin-right from here */
    /* margin-right: 0; */
  }

  /* Add a right border to all items EXCEPT the last one */
  .navbar-item:not(:last-child) {
    border-right: 1px solid #555; /* Subtle border color */
  }
```

```
.navbar-link {
  display: block; /* Use block display so padding/border work better
*/
  padding: 8px 15px; /* Add padding *inside* the item/link */
}
}
```

(Result: On wider screens, links are separated by a thin vertical border instead of just space.)

Personal Insight: Building responsive navigation is a fundamental exercise. Pay attention to how you handle spacing (margin vs. padding vs. gap in Flexbox/Grid, and making sure you remove spacing on the *last* item if using margins). Using `display: flex` on the `ul` is a common and clean way to arrange list items horizontally. The mobile-first approach here means the default stacked layout is defined first, then the horizontal Flexbox layout overrides it above a certain width.

Further Exploration:
- Add a site logo to the left and push the nav links to the right (use `margin-left: auto;` on the list within a flex container header, or put the logo and nav list in their own flex container).
- Implement a "hamburger" icon on mobile that toggles the visibility of the `.navbar-list` using CSS `display` and potentially a CSS transition or animation for the reveal/hide effect (this often requires a bit of JavaScript or clever CSS toggles like the checkbox hack, which is outside the scope of pure CSS layout but good to be aware of).
- Make the header "sticky" using `position: sticky;` (from Chapter 2).

10.2 Project 2: Crafting a Multi-Column Blog Layout
A classic blog layout often features a main content area and a sidebar (for author info, categories, ads, etc.). This is a perfect use case for CSS Grid because we're arranging elements in two dimensions: rows (header, content/sidebar, footer) and columns (main content and sidebar).

Goal: Create a layout with a header, footer, main content area, and a sidebar, which adapts from a single column stack on mobile to a multi-column layout on desktop.

Concepts Reinforced: CSS Grid (`display`, `grid-template-columns`, `grid-template-rows`, `gap`, `grid-area`, `grid-template-areas`), Responsiveness (Media Queries), Box Model, Basic Styling.

HTML Structure:

Semantic HTML elements are great for this: `header`, `main`, `aside`, `footer`. A container wraps them.

```html
<!-- Inside your body tag, below the nav -->
<div class="blog-layout-container">
  <header class="blog-header">
    <h1>Blog Title</h1>
  </header>
  <main class="blog-main-content">
    <h2>Post Title</h2>
    <p>This is the main content of the blog post...</p>
    <!-- Add more paragraphs or content here -->
    <p>End of main content.</p>
  </main>
  <aside class="blog-sidebar">
    <h3>Sidebar</h3>
    <p>Author info, categories, etc.</p>
  </aside>
  <footer class="blog-footer">
    <p>© 2023 Blog Name</p>
  </footer>
</div>
```

CSS Implementation (Step-by-Step):

Step 1: Base Styles (Mobile-First Stacked)

On mobile, we want the elements to stack vertically: Header, Main Content, Sidebar, Footer. We'll add basic styling and use Grid, but define it as a single column initially. We'll also name the grid areas for easier placement later.

```css
/* --- Project 2: Multi-Column Blog Layout --- */

.blog-layout-container {
  display: grid; /* Use Grid even on mobile */
  grid-template-columns: 1fr; /* Define a single column that takes
available space */
  grid-template-rows: auto auto auto auto; /* Rows sized based on
content */
```

```
  gap: 20px; /* Space between grid items/areas */
  padding: 20px; /* Padding around the layout */
  border: 2px solid teal; /* Outline for visualization */

  /* Name the grid areas for placement */
  grid-template-areas:
    "header"
    "main"
    "sidebar"
    "footer";
}


/* Assign elements to their named areas */
.blog-header     { grid-area: header;  background-color: #e0f2f7;
padding: 15px; text-align: center; }
.blog-main-content { grid-area: main;   background-color: #fff;
padding: 15px; }
.blog-sidebar    { grid-area: sidebar; background-color: #f0f0f0;
padding: 15px; }
.blog-footer     { grid-area: footer;  background-color: #e0f2f7;
padding: 15px; text-align: center; }
```

(Result: On all screen sizes, you'll see the four colored blocks stacked vertically with space between them, based on the single-column, four-row grid definition.)

Step 2: Desktop Layout with Two Columns

Now, we use a media query to redefine the grid for wider screens. We'll introduce two columns and rearrange the areas.

```
/* Add this *after* the base styles */


/* Media query for larger screens (e.g., 768px and up) */
@media (min-width: 768px) {
  .blog-layout-container {
    /* Redefine columns: 1fr for main, 250px for sidebar */
    grid-template-columns: 1fr 250px;
```

```
    /* Redefine rows: header (auto), main/sidebar area (1fr), footer
(auto) */
    /* Only 3 rows needed now as main and sidebar are in the same row
*/
    grid-template-rows: auto 1fr auto;

    /* Redefine the grid areas visually */
    grid-template-areas:
      "header  header"  /* Header spans both columns */
      "main    sidebar" /* Main in column 1, Sidebar in column 2 */
      "footer  footer"; /* Footer spans both columns */

    /* Optional: Adjust gap or padding for desktop */
    /* gap: 30px; */
  }


  /* No need to change grid-area property on items - they already know
their names! */
}
```

(Result: Below 768px, the layout is the stacked single column. At 768px and wider, the grid completely changes. The header and footer span across the two columns, and the main content sits to the left of the sidebar.)

Personal Insight: Using `grid-template-areas` makes redefining the layout with media queries incredibly clean and readable. You literally just redraw the grid in CSS. This pattern is excellent for main page layouts where the structure changes significantly across breakpoints. Notice how we didn't need to change the `grid-area` property on the items inside the media query – they respond automatically to the new area definitions on the container.

Further Exploration:

- Add more content to the main and sidebar columns to see how the `1fr` unit distributes space.
- Experiment with different column sizes (e.g., `2fr 1fr` to make the main content twice as wide as the sidebar, or using `minmax()` for the sidebar width).
- Use Flexbox *inside* the `blog-header` to arrange a logo and navigation horizontally.
- Add responsiveness to images within the main content using `max-width: 100%; height: auto;`.

10.3 Project 3: Building Interactive Product Cards

Product cards are a common UI pattern on e-commerce sites, blogs, or portfolios. They typically include an image, title, description, and perhaps a price or button. We'll focus on creating a basic card structure and adding subtle hover interactions using transitions and transforms.

Goal: Design a simple card component and add interactive visual feedback on hover.

Concepts Reinforced: Box Model, Basic Styling (Borders, Padding, Shadows, Colors), Transitions, Transforms (`scale`, `translate`), Pseudo-classes (`:hover`).

HTML Structure:

A `div` for the card container, containing an image, a heading, and a paragraph.

```html
<!-- Inside your body tag -->
<div class="product-card">
  <img src="https://via.placeholder.com/300x200" alt="Product Image"
class="card-image">
  <div class="card-content">
    <h3 class="card-title">Awesome Product</h3>
    <p class="card-description">This is a brief description of the
product.</p>
    <button class="card-button">View Details</button>
  </div>
</div>
```

(Note: Replace `https://via.placeholder.com/300x200` with a real image URL if you have one, or use a service like Placeholder.com to generate simple placeholder images.)

CSS Implementation (Step-by-Step):
Step 1: Basic Card Structure and Styling

Let's style the card container and its basic elements.

```css
/* --- Project 3: Interactive Product Cards --- */

.product-card {
  width: 300px; /* Fixed width for simplicity in this example */
  border: 1px solid #ddd;
  border-radius: 8px; /* Rounded corners */
```

```css
  overflow: hidden; /* Hide parts of the image if it exceeds border-
  radius */
  margin: 20px;     /* Space around the card */
  box-shadow: 0 4px 8px rgba(0, 0, 0, 0.1); /* Subtle shadow */
  background-color: white;
  text-align: center; /* Center content inside */

  /* Add transition for smooth hover effect */
  transition: transform 0.3s ease-in-out, box-shadow 0.3s ease-in-out;
}

.card-image {
  display: block; /* Ensure image doesn't have extra space below it */
  width: 100%;    /* Make image fill the card's width */
  height: auto;   /* Maintain aspect ratio */
}

.card-content {
  padding: 15px;
}

.card-title {
  font-size: 1.2em;
  color: #333;
  margin-top: 0;
  margin-bottom: 10px;
}

.card-description {
  font-size: 0.9em;
  color: #555;
  margin-bottom: 15px;
}

.card-button {
  background-color: #007bff;
  color: white;
  padding: 8px 15px;
  border: none;
```

```css
  border-radius: 4px;
  cursor: pointer;
  font-size: 1em;
  transition: background-color 0.3s ease; /* Smooth button color
change */
}


.card-button:hover {
  background-color: #0056b3;
}
```

(Result: A standard, well-styled card with an image, text, and a button.)

Step 2: Add Interactive Hover Effect

Now, let's make the entire card respond to hover using `transform` and the `transition` we already added to the container.

```css
/* Add this *after* the styles above */


.product-card:hover {
  /* Scale the card slightly */
  transform: scale(1.03);
  /* Enhance the shadow to give a lifted appearance */
  box-shadow: 0 8px 16px rgba(0, 0, 0, 0.2);
}
```

(Result: When you hover over the card, it smoothly scales up a little and the shadow darkens/expands, creating a nice interactive effect.)

Personal Insight: Interactive elements like these cards benefit greatly from subtle transitions and transforms. It provides immediate, intuitive feedback to the user that the element is interactive. The `scale()` transform is particularly effective for cards to make them feel like they are "popping" off the page slightly. Using `transition: all` or specifically listing the properties (`transform`, `box-shadow`) on the base state means the effect works both when hovering *on* and hovering *off*.

Further Exploration:
- Add a ribbon or badge to the corner of the card using `position: absolute;` (Chapter 2).
- Make the description text fade in or slide up slightly on hover using transitions or simple animations.
- Arrange multiple cards in a responsive grid using Flexbox or Grid (combining this project with Chapter 3 or 4).
- Use CSS variables (Chapter 8) for colors, spacing, and border radius to make the card easily themeable.

10.4 Project 4: Designing a Simple Photo Gallery

Creating grids of images is another common layout task. CSS Grid, especially with `repeat(auto-fit, minmax())` and `gap`, makes this much simpler and automatically responsive.

Goal: Create a responsive grid of images that adjusts the number of columns based on screen width.

Concepts Reinforced: CSS Grid (`display`, `grid-template-columns`, `gap`, `repeat`, `auto-fit`, `minmax`), Flexible Images, Box Model.

HTML Structure:

A container `div` holding several `img` elements (or `div`s containing images if you need more complex item styling).

```html
<!-- Inside your body tag -->
<div class="gallery-grid">
  <img
src="https://via.placeholder.com/300x200/FF5733/fff?text=Image+1"
alt="Gallery Image 1">
  <img
src="https://via.placeholder.com/300x200/33FF57/fff?text=Image+2"
alt="Gallery Image 2">
  <img
src="https://via.placeholder.com/300x200/3357FF/fff?text=Image+3">
  <img
src="https://via.placeholder.com/300x200/FF33A1/fff?text=Image+4">
  <img
src="https://via.placeholder.com/300x200/A133FF/fff?text=Image+5">
  <img
src="https://via.placeholder.com/300x200/33FFCE/fff?text=Image+6">
```

```
  <img
src="https://via.placeholder.com/300x200/FFC300/fff?text=Image+7">
  <img
src="https://via.placeholder.com/300x200/C70039/fff?text=Image+8">
</div>
```

(Note: Using different colored placeholder images helps visualize the grid layout.)

CSS Implementation (Step-by-Step):

Step 1: Set up the Grid Container and Gap

We'll use `display: grid;` and set a gap between the items.

```css
/* --- Project 4: Simple Photo Gallery --- */

.gallery-grid {
  display: grid; /* Activate Grid layout */
  gap: 15px;    /* Space between grid items */
  padding: 15px; /* Padding around the grid */
  border: 2px solid brown; /* Outline for visualization */
}

/* Make images flexible */
.gallery-grid img {
  display: block; /* Remove potential extra space below images */
  width: 100%;    /* Make image fill its grid cell width */
  height: auto;   /* Maintain aspect ratio */
  object-fit: cover; /* Optional: Ensure image covers its box without
distortion, might crop */
  /* Give images a minimum height if using object-fit cover and the
grid cell's height is flexible */
  min-height: 150px;
}
```

(Result: The images will likely stack vertically by default as we haven't defined columns yet. The `gap` will add space between them.)

Step 2: Define Responsive Columns with `repeat()` and `minmax()`

This is the key to the responsive photo gallery layout using Grid. We'll define columns that automatically adjust.

```css
/* Add this to the .gallery-grid rule */
.gallery-grid {
  display: grid;
  gap: 15px;
  padding: 15px;
  border: 2px solid brown;

  /* Define responsive columns:
      - Repeat automatically fitting columns
      - Each column should be AT LEAST 150px wide, but take up 1
  fraction of available space if more is there
  */
  grid-template-columns: repeat(auto-fit, minmax(150px, 1fr));

  /* Optional: Center the grid within its container if there's extra
  space */
  /* justify-content: center; */
}

.gallery-grid img {
  display: block;
  width: 100%;
  height: auto;
  object-fit: cover;
  min-height: 150px; /* Ensures a consistent row height even if images
  have different aspect ratios */
}
```

(Result: The images will now arrange themselves into a grid. As you resize the browser window, the number of columns will automatically increase or decrease based on how many 150px-wide items can fit. The `1fr` ensures they share the space equally within each row.)

Personal Insight: The `repeat(auto-fit, minmax(..., 1fr))` pattern is a powerful one-liner for creating responsive grids of items where you know the minimum size you want each item to be, but want them to fill the container flexibly. It's fantastic for galleries, product listings, or dashboards where the number of items per row needs to adapt automatically. The combination of `min-height` and `object-fit: cover` on the images themselves is useful for making gallery rows look tidy even if the source images have varied aspect ratios.

Further Exploration:

- Add a hover effect to the images (e.g., slight scale, change opacity, add border).
- Add a caption overlay that appears on hover (combine Grid/Flexbox for positioning the caption inside the item, and transitions for showing/hiding).
- Explore `auto-fill` vs `auto-fit` in the `repeat()` function to see the difference when there are fewer items than the maximum number of columns that could fit.
- Use Media Queries to set a larger minimum size for images on very large screens, or to explicitly set a fixed number of columns at certain breakpoints if you need more control than `auto-fit` provides.

10.5 Project 5: Creating a Dashboard Section Layout

Dashboards or complex application interfaces often require arranging multiple distinct panels or widgets into a structured layout. Grid is ideal for this, allowing you to define specific areas for different types of content and control how they span rows and columns.

Goal: Create a simple dashboard section layout with a main chart area, a list section, and a status box, arranged in a specific grid pattern.

Concepts Reinforced: CSS Grid (`display`, `grid-template-columns`, `grid-template-rows`, `gap`, `grid-area`, `grid-template-areas`), Responsiveness (Media Queries).

HTML Structure:

A container `div` holding `div` elements representing different dashboard panels.

```html
<!-- Inside your body tag -->
<div class="dashboard-layout">
  <div class="panel chart-panel">Chart Area</div>
  <div class="panel list-panel">List Section</div>
  <div class="panel status-panel">Status Box</div>
  <div class="panel activity-panel">Recent Activity</div>
</div>
```

CSS Implementation (Step-by-Step):
Step 1: Base Styles (Mobile-First Stacked) and Area Naming

Again, we start with a mobile-first approach, stacking the panels. We'll use Grid and define areas even though it's a single column.

```css
/* --- Project 5: Dashboard Section Layout --- */

.dashboard-layout {
  display: grid; /* Activate Grid */
  grid-template-columns: 1fr; /* Single column */
  grid-template-rows: auto auto auto auto; /* Rows based on content */
  gap: 20px;
  padding: 20px;
  border: 2px solid darkblue; /* Outline */

  /* Define grid areas for the stacked layout */
  grid-template-areas:
    "chart"
    "status" /* Status above list on mobile */
    "list"
    "activity"; /* Activity at the bottom */
}

/* Basic panel styling */
.panel {
  background-color: #fff;
  border: 1px solid #ccc;
  border-radius: 8px;
  padding: 15px;
  text-align: center; /* Center text within panels */
  min-height: 100px; /* Give panels a min-height for visualization */
}

/* Assign elements to named areas */
.chart-panel   { grid-area: chart;   background-color: lightblue; }
.list-panel    { grid-area: list;    background-color: lightgreen; }
.status-panel  { grid-area: status; background-color: lightcoral; }
.activity-panel{ grid-area: activity; background-color: lightyellow; }
```

(Result: On mobile, the panels stack vertically in the order: Chart, Status, List, Activity.)

Step 2: Desktop Layout with Grid Areas

For desktop, we'll redefine the grid to create a more complex 2D layout. Let's aim for something like:

- Top row: Chart spanning across
- Middle row: Status on the left, List and Activity on the right (List above Activity)
- No separate footer needed for this section, just panels.

```css
/* Add this *after* the base styles */

/* Media query for larger screens (e.g., 700px and up) */
@media (min-width: 700px) {
  .dashboard-layout {
    /* Redefine columns: Left column (e.g., 1fr), Right section (e.g.,
another 1fr) */
    grid-template-columns: 1fr 1fr;

    /* Redefine rows: Top row (chart), Middle row
(status/list/activity), optional bottom row */
    grid-template-rows: auto auto auto; /* Adjust if needed based on
desired complexity */

    /* Redefine grid areas VISUALLY */
    grid-template-areas:
      "chart   chart"    /* Chart spans both columns in the first row
*/
      "status  list"     /* Status in left column, List in right
column of the second row */
      ".       activity"; /* Empty cell in left column, Activity in
right column of the third row */
                          /* Or "status activity" if you want activity
next to status in the same row */
                          /* Or "status status" then "list activity" in
the next row */
                          /* Let's go with status/list next to each
other, then activity below list */
    grid-template-areas:
      "chart   chart"
      "status  list"
      "status  activity"; /* Status spans down 2 rows, List and
Activity are in the right column */
```

```
    /* Redefine grid template rows to match this area structure */
    grid-template-rows: auto 1fr 1fr; /* Chart row (auto),
Status/List row (1fr), Status/Activity row (1fr) */
  }


  /* No need to change grid-area on panels - they respond to the new
areas */
}
```

(Result: Below 700px, the panels stack. At 700px and wider, the layout changes dramatically. The Chart spans the top. The Status panel spans the left column across two rows. The List panel is in the top right, and the Activity panel is directly below it in the bottom right, filling the space next to the tall Status panel.)

Personal Insight: `grid-template-areas` truly shines for dashboard-like layouts where items have distinct roles and need precise placement and spanning. Changing the grid structure and areas within a media query allows for complex layout transformations with minimal CSS adjustments per item. Designing the layout visually with the area names is a powerful way to think about the structure.

Further Exploration:
- Experiment with different `grid-template-areas` definitions and `grid-template-rows`/`grid-template-columns` to create different dashboard layouts.
- Use `justify-items`, `align-items`, `justify-content`, `align-content` on the `.dashboard-layout` container or individual panels to control alignment within the grid or cells.
- Integrate simple content (like lists or small graphs) inside the panels and style them.
- Add borders or spacing within panels for a more polished look.

Conclusion: The Joy of Building
You've done it! You've moved from theory to practice, building foundational web components and layouts using modern CSS techniques.

Think back to where you started. You learned the language, how elements behave as boxes, how to arrange them in one dimension (Flexbox) and two (Grid), how to make those layouts adapt responsively across devices, how to style the visual elements, and add engaging motion. And now, you've applied these skills to build common patterns like navigation bars, blog layouts, product cards, image galleries, and dashboard sections.

The CSS journey is one of continuous learning and practice. The landscape evolves, new features are added, and new challenges arise with every project. But the fundamentals you've learned here – the Box Model, the Cascade, Specificity, Selectors, Flexbox, Grid, Media Queries – are the bedrock. They will serve you well for years to come.

These projects are just starting points. I encourage you to revisit them, tweak the styles, try different approaches, and integrate concepts from the "Advanced" and "Tools" chapters.

- Could you use CSS Variables for colors and spacing in the card or gallery projects? (Yes!)
- Could you use `clamp()` for fluid typography in the blog layout? (Absolutely!)
- Could you incorporate `mix-blend-mode` or `filter` for interesting visual effects in the gallery? (Definitely!)
- How would you use a preprocessor like Sass to manage the styles for these projects in a larger file structure?
- How would CSS Modules impact the way you write the CSS for the navigation bar or product card if they were part of a React application?

The best way to truly master CSS is to keep building. Find designs you like on the web and try to recreate their layout and styling from scratch. Take on small personal projects that require CSS. The more you code, experiment, and debug, the more intuitive it will become.

You now have the essential skills to tackle a wide range of web design challenges. Keep practicing, keep exploring, and most importantly, keep building! The power to make the web beautiful and functional is in your hands.

Chapter 11: Performance, Accessibility, and Best Practices

You've learned how to build layouts, style elements, make them responsive, and add interactivity. That's fantastic! But being a professional front-end developer isn't just about getting the visual output correct; it's also about building websites that are:

- **Performant:** Fast to load and smooth to interact with.
- **Accessible:** Usable by people of all abilities, including those using assistive technologies.
- **Maintainable & Scalable:** Easy for you and others to understand, modify, and build upon in the future.

These are not optional extras; they are fundamental qualities of a well-built website. Let's dive into how your CSS choices impact these critical areas.

11.1 Writing Maintainable and Scalable CSS Code

Remember how we talked about the global nature of CSS? This is the root cause of most maintainability and scalability problems. Without care, a CSS codebase can quickly become a tangled mess where changing one style accidentally breaks another (the dreaded "CSS Spaghetti" or "Cascade Hell").

Writing maintainable CSS means writing code that is:

- **Predictable:** You can look at a CSS rule and reasonably predict which elements it will affect and how it interacts with other styles.
- **Readable:** It's easy for anyone (including your future self!) to understand what the code is doing and why.
- **Modular:** Styles are grouped logically, often around components or features, reducing dependencies on the global scope.
- **Reusable:** Common patterns can be applied in multiple places without repeating code excessively.

Here's how we work towards that:

- **Organization:** As discussed in Chapter 9, having a clear file structure and grouping related styles is paramount. Whether you use a methodology like SMACSS (organizing by Base, Layout, Module, State, Theme), group by component (common in frameworks), or just have a consistent system for partials (`_variables.scss`, `_buttons.scss`, `_layout.scss`), consistency is key. Use imports in preprocessors or your build tool to combine them.
- **Consistency:** Establish and stick to a code style. This includes naming conventions (like BEM from Chapter 9), indentation, spacing, how you order properties within a rule, and how you write comments. A consistent style guide (even a simple one you create for yourself) makes code feel familiar and reduces cognitive load.

- **Meaningful Class Names:** Avoid generic names like `.box1`, `.item-right`. Use names that describe the *purpose* or *content* (`.product-card`, `.notification--error`, `.sidebar-toggle`). BEM is excellent at enforcing this semantic naming.
- **Limit Selector Specificity:** High specificity selectors (like `#id .container ul li a`) are hard to override later in the stylesheet, often forcing you to resort to more specific selectors or, worse, `!important`. Aim for lower, flatter specificity, typically relying on single class selectors (`.button`, `.card__title`) or combinations of classes (`.button--primary`). This makes styles easier to understand and override.
- **Use CSS Variables (Custom Properties):** As covered in Chapter 8, variables are essential for reusability and making global changes easy (theming).
- **Use Preprocessor Features (Mixins, Functions):** Mixins (Chapter 9) are great for abstracting and reusing blocks of declarations, reducing repetition.
- **Comment Your Code:** Explain *why* you did something, not just *what* you did (the code itself shows what you did). Explain complex rules, breakpoint logic, or workarounds for bugs.
- **Avoid `!important` (Generally):** We mentioned this in Chapter 1. While it has niche uses, frequent use of `!important` is a strong indicator that your specificity is out of control and your CSS architecture is becoming difficult to manage. It breaks the cascade and makes future overrides a nightmare.
- **Reduce Redundancy:** If you find yourself writing the same set of declarations repeatedly, look for ways to abstract it into a reusable class, a mixin, or use a more general selector combined with modifier classes.

Personal Insight: I've spent countless hours debugging stylesheets where specificity was out of control, comments were non-existent, and naming was inconsistent. It feels like navigating a maze built by someone who was actively trying to confuse you! Adopting consistent naming (BEM was a turning point for me) and using CSS variables (or preprocessor variables before they were common) were two of the biggest steps I took to make my own CSS, and the codebases I worked on, significantly more maintainable. You'll thank yourself later.

11.2 Optimizing CSS for Website Performance

CSS is a "render-blocking resource." This means that the browser usually pauses rendering the page until it has downloaded and processed all the CSS. If your CSS is slow to download or complex for the browser to parse, it directly impacts how quickly the user sees content ("Time to First Paint").

Here's how to make your CSS perform better:

- **Minimize File Size:**
  - **Minification:** Remove whitespace, comments, and shorten property/selector names (where safe). Build tools (Webpack, Parcel, Rollup) or dedicated tools (like cssnano, clean-css) do this automatically.

- o **Compression:** Serve CSS files compressed using Gzip or Brotli (configured on your web server).
- o **Remove Unused CSS:** As your project evolves, styles get added and sometimes removed from the HTML, but the old CSS hangs around. Tools like PurgeCSS can scan your HTML/templates and remove CSS rules that are not used, dramatically reducing file size.
- **Reduce HTTP Requests:** The fewer separate CSS files the browser has to download, the faster. Concatenate your CSS files into one or a few bundles (this is a standard feature of build tools and preprocessors).
- **Optimize Selector Performance (Less Critical Now, Still Relevant):** While modern browsers are very fast at matching selectors, extremely complex or inefficient selectors *can* still have a minor impact, especially on pages with a huge number of DOM elements. Avoid key selectors that are very general at the end of a long chain (e.g., `.module .list > li p span` - the browser has to check *every* `span` on the page to see if it matches). Simpler class selectors are generally faster.
- **Avoid Expensive Properties:** Some CSS properties require more computational work for the browser to render, especially if they change frequently (like in an animation).
  - o Properties that trigger layout recalculations or repaints of large areas (like `width`, `height`, `margin`, `padding`, `top`/`left` on `position: relative`/`absolute`) can be less performant to animate than...
  - o Properties that the browser can often handle more efficiently, typically on the GPU (`transform`, `opacity`, `filter`). As a rule of thumb, prefer animating `transform` and `opacity` when possible (as discussed in Chapter 7).
- **Critical CSS:** For very large sites, you might identify the minimum CSS required to render the visible part of the page ("above the fold") and inline that CSS directly into the `<head>` of your HTML. The rest of the CSS can be loaded asynchronously. This dramatically improves the perceived load speed. This is a more advanced optimization often handled by build processes.
- **Optimize Web Fonts:** As mentioned in Chapter 6, web fonts are extra downloads. Only load the weights and styles you need. Use modern formats (`woff2`). Consider font subsetting if you only need a specific character set. Use `font-display: swap;` or similar in `@font-face` or your Google Fonts link to prevent invisible text while the font loads.

Personal Insight: User patience for slow websites is near zero. A few hundred milliseconds can make a huge difference in bounce rates. While JavaScript and image optimization are often bigger culprits, unoptimized CSS can absolutely kill your initial page load performance. Leveraging build tools for minification and concatenation is non-negotiable. For image-heavy sites, tackling unused CSS can also provide a surprising speed boost.

11.3 Ensuring Accessibility with Semantic HTML and CSS

Accessibility (often shortened to A11y, because there are 11 letters between the A and the Y) means building websites that can be used by everyone, including people with disabilities (visual impairments, hearing impairments, mobility issues, cognitive disabilities, etc.). Accessibility is a fundamental web development responsibility.

CSS plays a vital role in accessibility, but it's also where mistakes can easily *break* accessibility.

- **Semantic HTML First:** CSS cannot fix fundamentally inaccessible HTML. Use appropriate HTML elements (`<nav>`, `<button>`, `<input type="checkbox">`, `<h1>`, `<p>`, `<aside>`, etc.) for their intended purpose. Don't use a `div` and try to make it look and behave exactly like a button using only CSS and JavaScript – the browser's native button has built-in accessibility features (keyboard navigability, roles for screen readers) that are hard to fully replicate.

- **Color Contrast:** We touched on this in Chapter 6. Ensure sufficient contrast between text and its background color for readability. Use online contrast checkers (like WebAIM Contrast Checker) to test color pairs against WCAG guidelines. Don't rely *only* on color to convey information (e.g., don't just make a required field's label red; add text like "(required)").

- **Focus Indicators:** When navigating with a keyboard (using the Tab key), the browser draws an outline around the currently focused element (`:focus` pseudo-class). **Do not remove this outline (`outline: none;`) unless you replace it with a clearly visible custom focus indicator.** Removing it is a major accessibility barrier for keyboard users. You can style the default outline, but don't remove it.

- **Text Resizing:** Users might zoom their browser or increase the default font size in their browser settings due to visual impairment. Using relative units (`rem`, `em`, `%`, `vw`, `vh`) for font sizes, padding, and margins (as discussed in Chapters 5 and 6) ensures that your layout and text scale correctly when the user adjusts font settings. Avoid fixed `px` values for layout that should adapt.

- **Responsive Design:** Making your layout usable and readable on small screens (Chapter 5) is crucial for people who might use mobile devices as their primary or only way to access the web.

- **Hiding Content Responsibly:** Using `display: none;` removes an element from the accessibility tree, meaning screen readers and other assistive technologies won't announce it. `visibility: hidden;` hides it visually but it *remains* in the accessibility tree and takes up space. If you need to visually hide content but keep it available for screen readers (e.g., "Skip to main content" links or labels for icons), use a CSS technique for visually hidden content that doesn't use `display: none;` or `visibility: hidden;` (often involves absolute positioning off-screen, zero size, and zero padding/border/margin).

- **ARIA Attributes:** ARIA (Accessible Rich Internet Applications) attributes are added to HTML to provide semantic meaning to elements that don't have it natively (e.g., making a custom `div`-based tab interface understandable to a screen reader). While these are HTML attributes (`role="tablist"`, `aria-selected="true"`), you will use CSS to style elements based on their ARIA attributes (e.g., `[aria-selected="true"] { font-weight: bold; }`), allowing you to visually represent the accessibility state.

Personal Insight: Building accessibly is not just a checkbox; it's about empathy. Imagine trying to use your website with just a keyboard, or listening to it through a screen reader. Testing with these tools (even basic keyboard navigation and browser accessibility features) is incredibly enlightening and quickly highlights areas for improvement. Making accessibility a habit from the start saves a ton of work down the line.

11.4 Tools for Linting and Formatting Your CSS

As your CSS codebase grows and involves multiple people, consistency in coding style becomes vital. Automated tools can enforce rules, catch errors, and automatically format your code.

- **Linters (e.g., Stylelint):** A linter analyzes your code for potential errors, stylistic inconsistencies, and adherence to best practices based on a configurable set of rules.
    - They can catch typos in property names or values.
    - They can enforce consistent units (e.g., always `rem` for font size).
    - They can limit nesting depth or prevent the use of `!important`.
    - They can flag selectors that are too specific.
    - You typically configure them with a ruleset (often based on community standards or team preferences). They integrate with code editors to show warnings/errors as you type and can be run as part of your build process to fail builds if rules are violated.
- **Formatters (e.g., Prettier):** A formatter automatically restyles your code according to a predefined set of rules (indentation, spacing, line breaks, semicolon usage, etc.).
    - You save the file, and the formatter instantly restructures the code to match the configured style.
    - This eliminates debates about minor style preferences in code reviews and ensures a consistent visual appearance across the entire codebase.
    - Prettier supports many languages, including CSS and SCSS/Less. It integrates with most popular code editors.

Personal Insight: Adopting a linter (Stylelint) and formatter (Prettier) was one of the single best things my teams have done for code quality and development speed. It automates the mundane tasks of code style review, freeing up code reviews to focus on logic and architecture. It means less time bikeshedding over spaces vs. tabs and more time building features. Highly, highly recommended.

11.5 Strategies for Cross-Browser Compatibility

Ah, the eternal challenge of front-end development! While modern browsers are better than ever at adhering to web standards, differences still exist:

- Different rendering engines (Blink in Chrome/Edge/Opera, WebKit in Safari, Gecko in Firefox).
- Users on older browser versions that don't support newer CSS features.
- Subtle differences in how browsers interpret complex specifications or handle edge cases.
- Vendor prefixes (less common for core features now, but still relevant for experimental or some animation properties in older browsers, e.g., `-webkit-`).

How do we build robust websites that work acceptably (or ideally, beautifully) across target browsers?

- **Define Target Browsers:** Understand which browsers and versions your users actually use (check analytics if available). You don't need to make your cutting-edge site look pixel-perfect in IE6, but you might need to support the last two versions of major browsers.
- **Test, Test, Test:** View your website on your target browsers and devices frequently during development. Emulating different devices in browser developer tools is a start, but testing on real devices is crucial. Automated testing tools can help check for layout regressions across browsers.
- **Use `caniuse.com`:** This website is an indispensable resource! Look up any CSS property or value to see exactly which browser versions support it. This helps you decide if you can use a feature or if you need fallbacks.
- **Provide Fallback Styles:** If you use a newer CSS feature not supported in older browsers, provide a simpler, supported style first. The browser will apply the first rule it understands and ignore the others.
    - Example: Solid background color before a gradient:
    - ```
      .element {
      ```
    - `    background-color: #007bff; /* Fallback: solid blue */`
    - `    background-image: linear-gradient(to right, blue, green);`
      `    /* Newer: gradient */`
      `}`

        Older browsers ignore `background-image` and get the solid color. Newer browsers apply the gradient, which overrides the `background-color`.

    - Example: Flexbox fallback (more complex): Before Flexbox, you might use `display: inline-block;` or floats. You could apply those first, then override with `display: flex;` in supported browsers.
      ```

- **Vendor Prefixes:** For some properties (especially newer or experimental ones), you might still need to include vendor-specific prefixes (`-webkit-`, `-moz-`, `-ms-`, `-o-`).
  - Example:
  - ```css
    .element {
      -webkit-transition: all 0.3s ease; /* Safari */
         -moz-transition: all 0.3s ease; /* Firefox */
          -ms-transition: all 0.3s ease; /* Internet Explorer */
           -o-transition: all 0.3s ease; /* Opera */
              transition: all 0.3s ease; /* Standard */
    }
    ```
  - *Personal Insight:* Manually adding and managing vendor prefixes is tedious and error-prone. **Do not do this by hand.** Tools like **Autoprefixer** (often used as a PostCSS plugin in build tools) read your standard CSS and automatically add the necessary vendor prefixes based on your desired browser support list (configured via `browserslist`). This is an essential part of a modern CSS build process.
- **Graceful Degradation vs. Progressive Enhancement:**
  - **Graceful Degradation:** Build the full experience for modern browsers first, then add fallbacks to make it work acceptably in older browsers.
  - **Progressive Enhancement:** Start with a solid, basic experience that works everywhere, then add enhancements (like advanced CSS features, rich interactions) that only work in modern browsers. This aligns well with the Mobile-First philosophy. Both are valid strategies depending on the project requirements and target audience.

Personal Insight: Cross-browser bugs are frustrating, but solvable. `caniuse.com` is your first stop. Testing is crucial, especially on actual mobile devices. Relying on tools like Autoprefixer saves you immense headaches with prefixes. And remember the fallback strategy – don't let a lack of support for one shiny new feature completely break the experience for a segment of your users.

Chapter 11 Summary

Mastering CSS isn't just about syntax; it's about building high-quality web experiences. In this chapter, you've learned:

- How to write **Maintainable and Scalable CSS** through organization, consistency, meaningful naming (like BEM), limiting specificity, using variables and mixins, and commenting.
    ```

- Strategies for **Optimizing CSS Performance**, including minification, compression, concatenation, removing unused code, and choosing performant properties (`transform, opacity`).
- The critical importance of **Accessibility (A11y)** and how to ensure your CSS supports it through good color contrast, focus indicators, responsive design, responsible content hiding, and using relative units for text scaling.
- Useful **Tools** like **Stylelint** (for linting/rules) and **Prettier** (for formatting) to automate code style and catch errors.
- Techniques for addressing **Cross-Browser Compatibility**, including testing, fallbacks, using `caniuse.com`, and automating vendor prefixes with tools like Autoprefixer.

These practices might seem like extra work at first, but they save immense time and effort in the long run, result in better products for your users, and are hallmarks of a skilled front-end developer. Make them a standard part of your workflow.

You've now covered the essential knowledge and practical techniques to write modern, effective, and responsible CSS. You understand how to style, layout, make responsive, add motion, leverage advanced features, and manage your code professionally.

This concludes the core instructional chapters. The path to mastery now lies in consistent practice and applying these techniques to real projects, continuously learning as the web platform evolves.

Conclusion: Continuing Your CSS Journey

Congratulations! If you've worked through the chapters and examples in this book, you've built a robust foundation in modern CSS. You are no longer a beginner just changing colors; you understand how to control layout, adapt designs to different devices, and make interfaces feel polished and interactive. That's a huge accomplishment!

Think back to the challenges we discussed early on – wrestling with layout, fighting the global scope, making things look good on different screens. You now have the knowledge and the tools to tackle these head-on. You're equipped to translate designs into code and build practical, usable websites.

But the world of web development is dynamic, and CSS is a living language that continues to evolve. To truly master CSS and remain effective throughout your career, you need to embrace ongoing learning.

Staying Up-to-Date in a Changing CSS Landscape

It's true, CSS isn't static! New properties, functions, selectors, and entire modules are being added all the time. Features that were experimental just a few years ago (like Grid and CSS Variables) are now standard. This constant evolution is exciting because it means CSS is becoming more powerful and capable, allowing us to build richer experiences directly in the browser.

So, how do you keep up without feeling overwhelmed?

- **Follow Key Resources:** Bookmark and regularly visit trusted websites that cover CSS updates. MDN Web Docs (developer.mozilla.org) is the official, authoritative reference – it's your best friend for looking up properties and seeing browser compatibility. Sites like CSS-Tricks (css-tricks.com) and Smashing Magazine (smashingmagazine.com) offer fantastic articles, tutorials, and news on the latest in CSS.
- **Follow Experts on Social Media:** Many developers who are deeply involved in CSS standards or are early adopters of new features share their knowledge on platforms like Twitter or Mastodon. Following them is a great way to catch announcements, see cool demos, and learn about best practices directly from the source.
- **Pay Attention to Browser Releases:** Major browser vendors (Chrome, Firefox, Safari, Edge) regularly release new versions with support for new CSS features. Following their release notes or blogs (like Chrome Developers or WebKit Blog) can give you a heads-up on what's coming.
- **Experiment in Dev Tools and Code Pens:** When you hear about a new feature, the fastest way to understand it is to try it out! Open up your browser's developer tools and experiment with changing values or adding properties. Platforms like CodePen or CodeSandbox are perfect for quickly trying out isolated CSS snippets.

- **Attend (or Watch) Talks:** Web conferences (even many free online ones) often feature talks on new or advanced CSS techniques. Watching recordings of these talks is a great way to see features explained and demonstrated by experts.

Personal Insight: I remember the feeling of trying to keep up when Flexbox and Grid were first becoming standard. It felt like a firehose of new information! My approach evolved from trying to learn *everything* about a new feature as soon as it was announced to focusing on understanding *what problem* it solves and *whether* it's relevant to my current projects. If it is, I dive in, read the MDN docs, find a good tutorial, and start experimenting. You don't need to memorize everything immediately; just know where to look when you need it. And remember that backward compatibility is a core principle of CSS, so your existing skills will still apply!

Community and Resources for Further Learning

You are not alone in your CSS journey! The web development community is incredibly active and helpful. Learning from others, asking questions, and eventually sharing your own knowledge are powerful ways to grow.

- **MDN Web Docs:** I'll mention it again because it's THAT important. It's the gold standard reference. Use it constantly.
- **CSS-Tricks and Smashing Magazine:** Essential reading for staying current and finding in-depth tutorials on specific topics.
- **Stack Overflow:** If you're stuck on a specific problem, chances are someone else has encountered it. Search Stack Overflow (and learn how to ask effective questions if you can't find an answer).
- **Reddit Communities:** Subreddits like `r/css`, `r/webdev`, and `r/frontend` are great places to see questions, learn from discussions, and share your own work.
- **Online Courses and Tutorials:** Many platforms offer courses that dive deeper into specific areas (like CSS Animations, advanced Grid techniques, or specific methodologies).
- **Developer Communities (Discord, Slack):** Many online learning platforms, podcasts, or web development groups have community chat servers where you can ask quick questions and connect with other developers.
- **Local Meetups and Conferences:** Connecting with developers in person (or virtually) is valuable for networking and learning about local trends and projects.

Don't be afraid to ask for help or admit when you don't know something. We've all been there! And as you grow, look for opportunities to help others – teaching is a fantastic way to solidify your own understanding.

Your Next Steps in Mastering CSS

Mastery comes through practice and application. Here's how you can continue building your CSS skills:

1. **Build More Projects:** The projects in this book are a starting point. Find website designs you admire and try to replicate them using the techniques you've learned. Start with simple components, then tackle full page layouts. This is the absolute best way to internalize the concepts.

2. **Focus on Real-World Problems:** As you build, you'll encounter challenges that aren't neatly covered in a tutorial. How do you handle variations of a component? How do you integrate with a specific JavaScript framework's styling approach? These are the moments where real learning happens.

3. **Dive Deeper:** Pick an area from the book that interests you or that you found challenging and explore it further. Maybe you want to truly master responsive images, dig into complex Grid layouts, build a full design system with CSS variables, or perfect your animation skills. There are entire books and courses dedicated to these specific topics.

4. **Integrate with JavaScript:** CSS rarely lives in isolation. Start integrating your CSS skills with JavaScript. Learn how to toggle classes based on user interaction or data, manage component-specific styles in frameworks (like CSS Modules, Styled Components, etc. – which weren't covered in depth here but are part of the ecosystem introduced in Chapter 9).

5. **Practice Performance & Accessibility:** Make performance testing and accessibility checks a standard part of your workflow for *every* project, no matter how small. It's easier to build them in from the start than to fix them later.

6. **Review and Refactor:** Look back at your own code after a few weeks or months. Can you improve it? Is it still readable? Refactoring is a key skill for writing maintainable CSS.

Personal Insight: My biggest leaps in CSS weren't from reading more books, but from building actual websites and applications. Each project presented new layout puzzles, performance bottlenecks, or styling challenges that forced me to go back to the docs, try new techniques, and truly understand *why* something worked (or didn't). Don't be afraid to struggle a bit; it's part of the process. Celebrate when you finally figure out that tricky alignment or get that animation to feel just right!

You have the fundamental knowledge. You understand the tools. You know where to find more information and how to keep learning. The most important step now is to keep applying what you know and keep building.

Thank you for choosing this book as your guide to practical CSS. I hope it has demystified CSS and empowered you to build beautiful, performant, and accessible websites.

Now, go forth and style the web!

Appendix: CSS Property and Selector Reference

This appendix serves as a concise lookup guide for the most common and essential CSS properties and selectors discussed throughout this book. It's not an exhaustive list of all CSS features, but a handy reference for the fundamental tools you've learned to build modern web interfaces.

Refer back to the relevant chapters for more detailed explanations and examples of how these are used in practice.

Key CSS Properties

Fundamentals & Box Model (Chapter 1)

- `width`, `height`
  - Sets the width or height of an element's content box (by default).
  - *Values:* `auto`, `length` (px, em, rem), `percentage`, `min-content`, `max-content`, `fit-content`.
- `padding` (shorthand)
  - Sets the space between an element's content and its border. Takes background color.
  - *Values:* `length`, `percentage`. Shorthand: `[top right bottom left]` or `[top/bottom left/right]` or `[all four]`. Individual properties: `padding-top`, `padding-right`, `padding-bottom`, `padding-left`.
- `border` (shorthand)
  - Sets the border of an element.
  - *Values:* `[width] [style] [color]`. E.g., `1px solid black`. Individual properties: `border-width`, `border-style`, `border-color`. Sides: `border-top`, `border-right`, `border-bottom`, `border-left`. Corner radius: `border-radius`.
- `margin` (shorthand)
  - Sets the space outside an element's border, pushing it away from other elements. Transparent.
  - *Values:* `auto`, `length`, `percentage`. Shorthand: `[top right bottom left]` or `[top/bottom left/right]` or `[all four]`. Individual properties: `margin-top`, `margin-right`, `margin-bottom`, `margin-left`.
- `box-sizing`
  - Defines how the `width` and `height` of an element are calculated (whether they include padding and border).
  - *Values:* `content-box` (default), `border-box`.

Basic Layout & Positioning (Chapter 2)

- `display`

- o Determines the type of box an element generates and how it interacts with other elements.
- o *Values:* block, inline, inline-block, none, flex, inline-flex, grid, inline-grid, etc.
- **position**
  - o Controls an element's positioning method. Used with top, right, bottom, left.
  - o *Values:* static (default), relative, absolute, fixed, sticky.
- **top, right, bottom, left**
  - o Offsets a *positioned* element from its normal position or its positioning context.
  - o *Values:* auto, length, percentage.
- **z-index**
  - o Sets the stack order of a *positioned* element. Higher values are closer to the user.
  - o *Values:* auto, integer.
- **overflow**
  - o Controls how content is handled when it exceeds the bounds of its container.
  - o *Values:* visible, hidden, scroll, auto. Can use overflow-x and overflow-y for individual axes.

Flexbox (Chapter 3 - Container Properties)

- **display**
  - o flex: Turns the element into a block-level flex container.
  - o inline-flex: Turns the element into an inline-level flex container.
- **flex-direction**
  - o Sets the direction of the main axis.
  - o *Values:* row, row-reverse, column, column-reverse.
- **flex-wrap**
  - o Controls whether flex items wrap onto new lines.
  - o *Values:* nowrap, wrap, wrap-reverse.
- **justify-content**
  - o Aligns flex items *along the main axis*.
  - o *Values:* flex-start, flex-end, center, space-between, space-around, space-evenly.
- **align-items**
  - o Aligns flex items *along the cross axis* within each line.
  - o *Values:* stretch, flex-start, flex-end, center, baseline.
- **align-content**
  - o Aligns the *lines* of flex items *along the cross axis* (requires flex-wrap: wrap).

- *Values:* `stretch, flex-start, flex-end, center, space-between, space-around, space-evenly`.
- **gap** (shorthand)
    - Sets the space between flex items. Also available as `row-gap` and `column-gap`.
    - *Values:* `length`.

Flexbox (Chapter 3 - Item Properties)

- **order**
    - Sets the visual order of a flex item.
    - *Values:* `integer`.
- **flex-grow**
    - Specifies how much a flex item grows relative to others when there's extra space.
    - *Values:* `number` (default 0).
- **flex-shrink**
    - Specifies how much a flex item shrinks relative to others when there's not enough space.
    - *Values:* `number` (default 1).
- **flex-basis**
    - Sets the initial size of a flex item before growing/shrinking.
    - *Values:* `auto, length, percentage`.
- **flex** (shorthand)
    - Shorthand for `flex-grow, flex-shrink,` and `flex-basis`.
    - *Values:* `[grow] [shrink] [basis]`. **Common:** `auto` (`1 1 auto`), `none` (`0 0 auto`), `1` (`1 1 0%`).
- **align-self**
    - Overrides `align-items` for a single flex item.
    - *Values:* `auto, stretch, flex-start, flex-end, center, baseline`.

CSS Grid (Chapter 4 - Container Properties)

- **display**
    - `grid`: Turns the element into a block-level grid container.
    - `inline-grid`: Turns the element into an inline-level grid container.
- **grid-template-columns, grid-template-rows**
    - Define the columns and rows of the grid and their sizes.
    - *Values:* `length, percentage, auto, fr` (fraction), `min-content, max-content, minmax(min, max), repeat()`.
- **gap** (shorthand)
    - Sets the space between grid items (tracks). Also available as `row-gap` and `column-gap`.

- o *Values:* length.
- **grid-template-areas**
  - o Defines grid areas and assigns them names visually.
  - o *Values:* Strings representing rows, with area names or . for empty cells.
- **justify-items**
  - o Aligns grid items *along the inline axis* (horizontal) within their cells.
  - o *Values:* start, end, center, stretch.
- **align-items**
  - o Aligns grid items *along the block axis* (vertical) within their cells.
  - o *Values:* start, end, center, stretch, baseline.
- **place-items** (shorthand)
  - o Shorthand for align-items justify-items.
  - o *Values:* [align-items value] [justify-items value] or [single value] for both.
- **justify-content**
  - o Aligns the *entire grid* along the *inline axis* if the grid is smaller than the container.
  - o *Values:* start, end, center, space-between, space-around, space-evenly, stretch.
- **align-content**
  - o Aligns the *entire grid* along the *block axis* if the grid is smaller than the container.
  - o *Values:* start, end, center, space-between, space-around, space-evenly, stretch.
- **place-content** (shorthand)
  - o Shorthand for align-content justify-content.
  - o *Values:* [align-content value] [justify-content value] or [single value] for both.

CSS Grid (Chapter 4 - Item Properties)
- **grid-column-start, grid-column-end**
  - o Define which vertical grid lines an item starts and ends at.
  - o *Values:* integer (line number), span count, span identifier, auto.
- **grid-row-start, grid-row-end**
  - o Define which horizontal grid lines an item starts and ends at.
  - o *Values:* integer (line number), span count, span identifier, auto.
- **grid-column, grid-row** (shorthands)
  - o Shorthands for start/end lines.
  - o *Values:* [start] / [end] or [start] / span [count].
- **grid-area** (for placement by name)
  - o Places a grid item into a named grid area.

o *Values:* name (from grid-template-areas). Can also be a shorthand for line placement: [row-start] / [column-start] / [row-end] / [column-end].

- **justify-self**
  - o Overrides justify-items for a single grid item (inline axis).
  - o *Values:* auto, start, end, center, stretch.
- **align-self**
  - o Overrides align-items for a single grid item (block axis).
  - o *Values:* auto, start, end, center, stretch, baseline.
- **place-self** (shorthand)
  - o Shorthand for align-self justify-self.
  - o *Values:* [align-self value] [justify-self value] or [single value] for both.

Typography & Text (Chapter 6)

- **font-family**
  - o Sets the typeface. List fallback fonts.
  - o *Values:* Comma-separated list of font names and generic families (serif, sans-serif, etc.).
- **font-size**
  - o Sets the size of the text.
  - o *Values:* length (px, em, **rem**, vw, vh), percentage, keywords.
- **font-weight**
  - o Sets the thickness of text.
  - o *Values:* normal, bold, 100-900, etc.
- **font-style**
  - o Sets text to italic.
  - o *Values:* normal, italic.
- **line-height**
  - o Sets the height of lines of text.
  - o *Values:* normal, number (unitless multiplier), length, percentage.
- **text-align**
  - o Aligns inline content within its block container horizontally.
  - o *Values:* left, right, center, justify.
- **text-decoration**
  - o Adds or removes lines on text.
  - o *Values:* none, underline, overline, line-through.
- **text-transform**
  - o Changes casing.

- o *Values:* none, uppercase, lowercase, capitalize.
- **letter-spacing**, **word-spacing**
  - o Adjusts space between letters or words.
  - o *Values:* normal, length.

Color & Backgrounds (Chapter 6)

- **color**
  - o Sets the foreground color (text color).
  - o *Values:* Named colors, Hex, RGB(A), HSL(A), var().
- **background-color**
  - o Sets the solid background color.
  - o *Values:* Named colors, Hex, RGB(A), HSL(A), var().
- **background-image**
  - o Sets one or more background images or gradients.
  - o *Values:* none, url(...), linear-gradient(...), radial-gradient(...), comma-separated list.
- **background-repeat**
  - o Controls image tiling.
  - o *Values:* repeat, no-repeat, repeat-x, repeat-y. Can list values for multiple backgrounds.
- **background-position**
  - o Sets image starting position.
  - o *Values:* Keywords (top, center, bottom, left, right), length, percentage. Can list values for multiple backgrounds.
- **background-size**
  - o Sets image size.
  - o *Values:* auto, cover, contain, length, percentage. Can list values for multiple backgrounds.
- **background-attachment**
  - o Image scrolls with element or is fixed to viewport.
  - o *Values:* scroll, fixed, local. Can list values for multiple backgrounds.
- **background** (shorthand)
  - o Shorthand for background properties. Order matters for size after position (position/size).
  - o *Values:* [color] [image] [repeat] [attachment] [position] / [size] [origin] [clip]. Can list comma-separated sets for multiple backgrounds.

Motion & Interaction (Chapter 7 - Transitions)

- **transition-property**
  - Which properties to transition.
  - *Values:* `none`, `all`, specific `property-name`, comma-separated list.
- **transition-duration**
  - How long the transition takes.
  - *Values:* `time` (s, ms).
- **transition-timing-function**
  - The speed curve of the transition.
  - *Values:* `ease`, `linear`, `ease-in`, `ease-out`, `ease-in-out`, `cubic-bezier(...)`, `steps(...)`.
- **transition-delay**
  - Delay before transition starts.
  - *Values:* `time` (s, ms).
- **transition** (shorthand)
  - Shorthand for transition properties.
  - *Values:* `[property] [duration] [timing-function] [delay]`, comma-separated for multiple transitions.

Motion & Interaction (Chapter 7 - Transforms)

- **transform**
  - Applies geometric transformations.
  - *Values:* `none`, `translate()`, `rotate()`, `scale()`, `skew()`, `translateX()`, `translateY()`, `translateZ()`, `rotateX()`, `rotateY()`, `rotateZ()`, `scaleX()`, `scaleY()`, `scaleZ()`, `translate3d()`, `rotate3d()`, `scale3d()`, `matrix()`, `matrix3d()`, `perspective()`. Can list multiple functions space-separated.
- **transform-origin**
  - Point around which transforms occur.
  - *Values:* `[x-position] [y-position] [z-position]`. x/y values: `left`, `center`, `right`, `top`, `bottom`, `length`, percentage. z value: `length`. Default is `center center`.

Motion & Interaction (Chapter 7 - Animations)

- **@keyframes**
  - Rule to define an animation sequence.
  - *Syntax:* `@keyframes animation-name { 0% { ... } 50% { ... } 100% { ... } }` (or from/to).
- **animation-name**
  - The name of the `@keyframes` rule to use.

- o *Values:* none, `keyframe-name`, comma-separated list.
- **animation-duration**
  - o How long one cycle takes.
  - o *Values:* `time` (s, ms).
- **animation-timing-function**
  - o The speed curve of the animation.
  - o *Values:* Same as `transition-timing-function`.
- **animation-delay**
  - o Delay before animation starts.
  - o *Values:* `time` (s, ms).
- **animation-iteration-count**
  - o How many times to repeat.
  - o *Values:* `number`, `infinite`.
- **animation-direction**
  - o Whether to play forwards/backwards/alternate.
  - o *Values:* `normal`, `reverse`, `alternate`, `alternate-reverse`.
- **animation-fill-mode**
  - o Styles applied before/after animation.
  - o *Values:* `none`, `forwards`, `backwards`, `both`.
- **animation-play-state**
  - o Running or paused.
  - o *Values:* `running`, `paused`.
- **animation** (shorthand)
  - o Shorthand for animation properties.
  - o *Values:* `[name] [duration] [timing-function] [delay] [iteration-count] [direction] [fill-mode] [play-state]`, comma-separated for multiple animations.

Advanced Features (Chapter 8)

- **CSS Variables (Custom Properties)**
  - o Defining: `--custom-property-name: value;` (e.g., `--primary-color: blue;`)
  - o Using: `var(--custom-property-name);` (e.g., `color: var(--primary-color);`)
- **calc()**
  - o Performs calculations.
  - o *Syntax:* `calc(expression)` (e.g., `width: calc(100% - 20px);`)
- **min()**
  - o Selects the smallest value.

- o *Syntax:* `min(value1, value2, ...)` (e.g., `width: min(500px, 50%);`)
- **max()**
  - o Selects the largest value.
  - o *Syntax:* `max(value1, value2, ...)` (e.g., `width: max(200px, 50%);`)
- **clamp()**
  - o Constrains a value between a min and max, scaling fluidly in between.
  - o *Syntax:* `clamp(min, preferred, max)` (e.g., `font-size: clamp(1rem, 2vw + 0.5rem, 2rem);`)
- **filter**
  - o Applies graphical effects.
  - o *Values:* `none`, `blur()`, `brightness()`, `contrast()`, `grayscale()`, `hue-rotate()`, `invert()`, `opacity()`, `sepia()`, `saturate()`, `drop-shadow()`, space-separated list.
- **mix-blend-mode**
  - o Blends element content with stack below.
  - o *Values:* `normal`, `multiply`, `screen`, `overlay`, `darken`, `lighten`, etc.
- **background-blend-mode**
  - o Blends background layers with each other and element background.
  - o *Values:* Same as `mix-blend-mode`.

Key CSS Selectors & Pseudo-classes

Basic Selectors (Chapter 1)

- *****
  - o Selects all elements (Universal Selector).
- **element**
  - o Selects all elements of a specific type (Type/Element Selector). E.g., `p`, `div`, `h1`.
- **.class**
  - o Selects all elements with a specific class attribute (Class Selector). E.g., `.button`, `.card-title`.
- **#id**
  - o Selects the *single* element with a specific id attribute (ID Selector). E.g., `#site-header`.
- **[attribute]**
  - o Selects all elements with a specific attribute (Attribute Selector). E.g., `[required]`.
- **[attribute="value"]**
  - o Selects all elements with a specific attribute and value. E.g., `[type="text"]`.
- **[attribute~="value"]**

- Selects elements with a specific attribute whose value is a space-separated list containing the given value. E.g., `[class~="button"]` (selects element if 'button' is one of its classes).
- **`[attribute^="value"]`**
  - Selects elements with a specific attribute whose value begins with the given value. E.g., `[href^="#"]` (selects internal page links).
- **`[attribute$="value"]`**
  - Selects elements with a specific attribute whose value ends with the given value. E.g., `[src$=".png"]` (selects PNG images).
- **`[attribute*="value"]`**
  - Selects elements with a specific attribute whose value contains the given value anywhere. E.g., `[alt*="logo"]` (selects images whose alt text contains 'logo').

Combinators (Chapter 1 - Implicitly used)

- **`selector1 selector2`**
  - Selects `selector2` elements that are descendants of `selector1` (Descendant Combinator). E.g., `.card p`.
- **`selector1 > selector2`**
  - Selects `selector2` elements that are *direct children* of `selector1` (Child Combinator). E.g., `.navbar-list > li`.
- **`selector1 + selector2`**
  - Selects the `selector2` element that is the *immediately adjacent sibling* of `selector1` (Adjacent Sibling Combinator). E.g., `h2 + p` (selects the paragraph immediately following an h2).
- **`selector1 ~ selector2`**
  - Selects all `selector2` elements that are siblings of `selector1` and come *after* it (General Sibling Combinator). E.g., `h2 ~ p` (selects all paragraphs that are siblings of an h2 and come after it).

Pseudo-classes (Various Chapters)

- **`:hover`**
  - Selects an element when the user hovers over it (typically with a mouse pointer). (Chapter 7)
- **`:focus`**
  - Selects an element when it has received focus (e.g., clicked, tabbed to). Crucial for accessibility. (Chapter 11)
- **`:active`**
  - Selects an element while it is being activated by the user (e.g., pressed down by mouse/finger). (Chapter 7)
- **`:visited`**
  - Selects a link (`<a>`) that the user has already visited. (Chapter 6 - implicitly)

- **:first-child, :last-child**
  - Selects an element that is the first or last child of its parent. E.g., `.navbar-item:last-child`. (Chapter 1, 10)
- **:nth-child(n)**
  - Selects an element that is the nth child of its parent. `n` can be a number, a keyword (`odd`, `even`), or a formula (`2n+1`). (Chapter 1 - implicitly)
- **:not(selector)**
  - Selects an element that does *not* match the given selector. E.g., `li:not(:last-child)`. (Chapter 8, 10)
- **:is(selector-list)**
  - Matches an element that matches any selector in the list. Specificity is that of the most specific argument. (Chapter 8)
- **:where(selector-list)**
  - Matches an element that matches any selector in the list. Always has zero specificity. (Chapter 8)
- **:has(selector-list)**
  - Selects the subject element *only if* it contains an element matching one of the selectors in the list. (Chapter 8)
- **::before, ::after**
  - Selects a pseudo-element that is the first/last child of an element. Used to insert cosmetic content via the `content` property. (Chapter 1 - implicitly, often used with Transforms/Animations in Chapter 7)

This reference appendix should provide a handy quick guide as you continue to build projects and reinforce your CSS skills. Happy coding!